ADVICE FROM THE DIAMOND HEADACHE CLINIC

ADVICE FROM THE DIAMOND HEADACHE CLINIC

by

Seymour Diamond, M.D.
and
Judi Diamond-Falk

INTERNATIONAL UNIVERSITIES PRESS, INC.
New York

Library of Congress Cataloging in Publication Data

Diamond, Seymour, 1925-
Advice from the Diamond Headache Clinic.

Bibliography: p.
Includes index.
1. Headache. I. Diamond-Falk, Judi. II. Title.
[DNLM: 1. Headache—Popular works. WL 342 D537a]
RC392.D495   1982   616.8′49   82-8973
ISBN 0-8236-0119-6   AACR2

Manufactured in the United States of America

To
Elaine Diamond,
whose tolerance, understanding, and critique
made this book possible.

CONTENTS

ACKNOWLEDGMENTS

We would like to thank Mary Franklin Epstein and Norma Jean McEwen, for their assistance in preparing the manuscript; Susan Snow, Jean Kemp, Ticla Lichtman, and Marilyn Long of the Dietary Department of Bethany Methodist Hospital in Chicago, for their help with the dietary portions of the book; Yvonne Manley, for her help with editing the manuscript; and Martin V. Azarian and Margaret Azarian, for their encouragement and support.

1

HEADACHES: THEIR CAUSES AND THEIR CURES

What Is a Headache?

"There is a disease which though it occurs very frequently, has not yet obtained a place in the systematic catalogues. It is commonly to be met with in practice and is described by those who are affected with it, and who are not few in number, under the compound title of 'sick headache.' " This was read to the Royal College of Physicians on December 14, 1778 by John Fothergill.[1]

Headache has been called the most common medical complaint and a universal medical problem. Recurring headaches may afflict half of the people in the world. It has been estimated that 42 million Americans suffer from severe, recurring headaches. Headache of some description will hit most people at some time in their life. Stress is probably the most common cause of headache because the individual tends to build an environment that is too great for him to handle.

A headache is a feeling of pain or discomfort in some part

[1] Quoted from *The Works of John Fothergill, M.D.*, by John Coakley Lettsom (London: Charles Dilly).

of the head. It can be a throbbing pain or a steady one. The pain can be mild enough to be ignored or it can be incapacitating. Cephalalgia, or headache, has been described as a feeling of dizziness, tenseness, an unusual sensation, or just a feeling of pressure, rather than actual pain. The different causes of the headache do not affect the severity of the pain. Those accompanying very serious illnesses are often mild in intensity, while those resulting from some benign medical problems are often very severe.

Headache pain is a symptom rather than a disease, which may account for the singular lack of interest accorded it in the past. It may signify a problem characterized by the headache itself, or an injury or malfunction, or it may be secondary to another condition. Some conditions involving headache as a symptom rather than the major problem include low blood sugar, hangover, fever, allergic reaction, and circulatory, glandular, and dental disease. Almost any medical disorder can provoke a headache.

The proliferation of headaches, especially among the young, is a symptom of the nature of our society as well as the individual. Our modern world is rampant with tension, frustration, anxiety, depression, and repressed hostility, all of which are "triggers" of headache pain. A multitude of chronic, recurring headaches are precipitated by stress.

Headaches can be classified by their pain-causing mechanism. This is not the underlying condition, but the immediate cause of pain. Various physical and neurological changes cause pain in different areas of the brain. One type of headache occurs in the blood vessels when they swell and rub on sensitive nerves, another occurs when muscles are pulled tight, and others involve the inflammation of tissues or membranes surrounding the brain. There are four mechanisms that can be involved—vasodilation, internal traction, inflammation, and muscle contraction. However, headaches with more than one cause are not uncommon.

Vasodilation

The first mechanism is vasodilation. The blood vessels or arteries inside and outside the skull dilate or expand; thus the walls of the blood vessels apply pressure on the accompanying nerve and cause pain. Vasodilation provokes the headache phase in vascular headaches. These include classic and common migraine, hemiplegic and ophthalmoplegic migraine, cluster, toxic, and hypertensive headaches. Other causes include changes in the chemical composition of the blood (carbon dioxide poisoning), fever, and some drug reactions. Vasodilation itself does not produce a headache, but may be accompanied by a local inflammation.

Internal Traction

The second mechanism—internal traction—is an indication of the presence of something foreign, such as a tumor or other growth, abscess, infection, swelling, or hematoma. The pain stems from the stress of pulling on the arteries.

Inflammation

Inflammation is the third mechanism that causes headaches. When tissues are injured or irritated, they become inflamed. Inflamed tissues are often characterized as being swollen, red, and warm. Inflammatory headaches accompany diseases of the eyes, ears, nose, teeth, sinuses, disorders of the neck and jaw, and neuralgias. Also included are those headaches due to inflammation in the membranes around the brain. Internal traction and inflammatory headaches are those caused by organic diseases. Although they are an infrequent cause of headache, prompt treatment is necessary.

Muscle Contraction

The fourth mechanism causing head pain is muscle contraction. Headaches can be caused by the tightening of

muscles, primarily of the neck, and secondarily of the face
and scalp. When muscles are tensed for a long period of time,
pain results in the form of a muscle contraction headache. It
is usually caused by worry, anxiety, a deep, prolonged depression, or poor posture. Physicians used to call muscle contraction headaches "psychogenic headaches," as they are usually
caused by anxiety or depression. They originate in the
"psyche."

How Is Pain Perceived?

Pain Threshold

The pain threshold is the level of sensitivity to pain. It
is the degree of discomfort an individual feels from a sensation
that causes him to perceive it as painful. The level at which
pain is felt varies from person to person, and even from situation to situation with the same person. Biological and emotional factors can play a role in one's pain threshold. A previous
injury to a particular area can lower the pain threshold. Depression, anxiety, and frustration also can lower it, while happiness
and contentment often raise it. Methods of raising the pain
threshold include distraction, suggestion, hypnosis, and medications such as analgesics and tricyclic antidepressants. Children generally have higher pain thresholds than adults.

Measurement of Pain

Headaches are a very subjective phenomenon. Pain is
subjective, as it is only experienced by the sufferer. The degree
of pain felt by another individual is difficult to assess. It is
necessary to rely on the sufferer's description for diagnosis of
the headache and determination of its severity, even though
some severe headaches do have various outward signs such
as nausea, vomiting, pallor, and sweating. Unfortunately, there

are no defined standards as to what pain is, so it cannot be measured by any reliable standard.

Pain Pathways

Pain is the primary symptom of most diseases. It serves the purpose of alerting the person to the fact that there is a problem and usually is a protective mechanism of the body for avoiding damage to itself. When the sensation of pain is constant and great, it transforms from a warning device to an alarm.

Pain is a message that is transmitted along nerve pathways, the nerve endings in the skin and internal organs, and received by the brain, which interprets it. The term "imaginary pain" has no meaning since all pain is "in the mind." It exists because the brain interprets all stimuli. The causes and types of pain differ in different parts of the body. Most nerves in the body can emit the pain sensation. The frequency of the nerve fiber discharges must increase to a rapid pace, leading to the feeling of pain. There are specialized nerve fibers that deliver the message of pain. The pain sensation at nerve endings is also activated by pain-causing chemicals released in the tissues. These vasoactive substances can cause the dilation of small blood vessels. Pain is regularly associated with inflammation.

The brain itself feels no pain, nor does the bone of the skull. The pain pathways from the head and neck come from the nerves supplying the skin, scalp, muscles, joints, skull, and membranes lining the brain. Even though the brain is not sensitive to pain, the nerves and blood vessels around the brain, the muscles in the head and neck, and the coverings around the brain do feel pain. Organs such as the eyes, ears, nose, mouth, and sinuses can be included as sources of head pain. The nerve fibers that are responsible for sensations in the scalp, muscles, and bones of the neck and skull can send the head

pain messages. However, the pain message more often originates in the arteries that supply the face, scalp, and brain with
blood. The fine nerve plexus in the walls of the arteries is very
sensitive to stretching.

The trigeminal nerve is the largest of the nerves responsible for sensations from the face and the front portion of the
scalp. Irritation of the trigeminal nerve causes pain in the jaw,
cheek, or forehead. It is also responsible for sensations coming
from the blood vessels in the brain and scalp. Headaches are
most often caused by the dilation of these blood vessels. When
an artery dilates, it causes the nerve fibers around it to stretch
and leads to a ''throbbing'' headache. The arteries of the scalp
are mainly responsible for headaches like migraine. Any pain
in the front half of the head results from activity in the trigeminal nerve, while any pain from the back half is derived
from spinal nerves which run through the back of the head and
join the upper part of the spinal cord. The neck, or cervical,
nerves carry painful sensations from the neck and back of the
head into the spinal cord and up to the cerebral hemispheres.
Another phenomenon that must be considered with headache
problems is that of referred pain. Discomfort originating in
one area may be perceived as coming from another area.

Nerves respond to heat, cold, pressure, and touch, as well
as pain. Excessive degrees of any of these stimuli can result
in painful sensations. Examples include the ''ice cream'' headache and the ''hat band'' headache (see Chapter 3). Anyone
can get a ''normal'' headache if the nerve supply to the blood
vessels or other structures of the head is stimulated excessively.

Psychological Factors

Although pain sensations remain fairly constant, people's
reactions to pain do not. People vary in their tolerance for
pain. Both physical and psychological factors affect pain tolerance. The mind influences the way one recognizes and in-

terprets a painful sensation. Some of the intervening factors include early conditioning (both personal and cultural), excitement or involvement, expectations, and surrounding situations. Psychological factors such as past experience, attention, and emotion also influence one's response to and perception of pain. Pain perception varies from person to person due to personality variables and cultural attitudes toward pain. Some reactions are influenced by the individual's background and are under voluntary control. Some people dwell on their symptoms and pain while others consciously or unconsciously suppress them. Social, emotional, and cultural influences affect one's interpretation of pain and method of dealing with it—either in the direction of encouraging demonstration of suffering or discouraging such expression. The emphasis on headache and sickness varies among people, with some becoming unable to work and totally incapacitated while others continue with their normal activities in a stoic manner.

One's level of attention and emotional response to the particular situation can influence how much pain is felt. Emotional factors can play a role in determining the amount of distress a headache causes. Fear can intensify the pain. Fear that the headache stems from a serious disorder adds to the frustration and anxiety of the sufferer.

Thus, the importance of knowledge and understanding of the individual's headache is emphasized, leading to greater relaxation and a reduction in the headache's intensity. Pain and anxiety feed on each other. Anxiety, depression, and agitation significantly increase the sensation of pain. Frustration and isolation accompany the head pain. The headache sufferer generally gets very little sympathy or compassion from others; many people cannot comprehend the degree of suffering that a headache can cause. Others conclude that since a headache is "all in the mind" the pain cannot be very severe or has been exaggerated.

Pain can become chronic, in which case it is transformed

from a symptom to a disease in itself. When there is head pain, the entire body suffers. Headaches can start in childhood and remain with one for one's entire life, thus becoming a part of one's identity and personality. Most headache patients show some "learned" pain. There are headache sufferers who *use* their pain to manipulate people and events. They can control their environment with their headaches. They may not be genuinely motivated to rid themselves of their headaches. Family members must learn to discourage "pain behavior" and reinforce normal behavior. Severe, recurring pain can lead to further problems such as drug dependency, depression, and disability. It is necessary to identify the origin of the pain and the factors contributing to the pain, and attempt to measure the severity of the pain in order to exercise control over a headache problem.

2

HISTORY OF HEADACHE DIAGNOSIS AND TREATMENT

At the time of the Egyptian dynasties, headache was believed to be due to the possession of evil spirits. The ancient Egyptians called the evil spirit of headache "Tiu" and believed that if one developed this type of headache, one was a broken person. They likened it to insanity.

Although the ancient Greeks were astute enough to develop a democratic type of government, their religion was based on fear. It was believed that the gods were able to inflict or remove disease at their will. And thus, the gods were blamed for the headaches of Greek citizens. About 400 B.C., Hippocrates described a type of headache which was very similar to the migraine syndrome. He gave a clear description of the warning, or aura, of classical migraine and the intense pain, as well as describing the relief that occurred with vomiting: "Most of the time [the patient] seemed to see something shining before him like a light, usually in part of the right eye; at the end of a moment, a violent pain supervened in the right temple, then in all the head and neck, where the head is attached to the spine . . . vomiting, when it became possible, was able to divert the pain and render it more moderate."[1] The ancient Jewish Talmud recommended that one rub the head with wine, vinegar, or oil to treat a headache. It is said in the Talmud: "I can tolerate any illness, but not an intestinal disease, any suffering, but not stomach or [heart] troubles, any pain, but not headache."[2]

The first person to classify headaches, and to describe the particular headache we now recognize as migraine, was Aretaeus of Cappadocia (100 A.D.). Aretaeus classified headaches into acute and chronic categories and distinguished migraine from daily headaches—muscle contraction headaches. An Aretaeus account of migraine, which he called "heterocrania," was as follows:

> But in certain cases, the parts of the right side, or those on the left solely . . . the pain does not pass this limit, but remains in the half of the head. This is called heterocrania, an illness by no means mild . . . if at any time it sets in acutely, it occasions unseemly and dreadful symptoms . . . nausea, vomiting of bilious matters, collapse of the patient, but if . . . it becomes chronic, there is much torpor, heaviness of the head, anxiety and weariness. They flee the light; the darkness soothes their disease; nor can they bear readily to look upon or hear anything disagreeable; their sense of smell is vitiated. Neither does anything agreeable to smell delight them, and they also have an aversion to fetid things; the patients, moreover, are weary of life, and wish to die. . . . The cause of these symptoms is coldness with dryness.[3]

Migraine was also described by the Greek physician

[1] Hippocrates, *Ober dicta* (400 B.C.).

[2] Julius Preuss, *Biblical and Talmudic Medicine*, translated and edited by Fred Rosner (New York/London: Sanhedrin Press, 1978), Chapter 10 (Neurological Disorders).

[3] Aretaeus, *The Extant Works of Aretaeus the Cappadocian*, edited by Francis Adams (London: Sydenham Society).

Galen, who lived 130–200 A.D. Galen was a great physiologist and anatomist, and, in particular, was noted for his drawings and writings on the nervous system. He was considered the founder of experimental physiology, and he introduced the word "hemicrania," or half the head. This term was gradually modified through the years to hemigrania, emigrania, migranea, megrim, and finally to its present form, migraine. According to Galen, "Hemicrania is a painful disorder affecting approximately one half of the head, either the right or left side, and which extends along the length of the longitudinal suture. This was due to ascent of vapours, either excessive in amount or too hot or too cold."[4]

Galen described the vascular connections between extracranial and intracranial circulation, that is, circulation within the brain itself and outside the brain. He thought that the source of headache was a disturbance in various parts of the body that dispatched liquids or vapors containing harmful properties to the brain. He wrote that the vomiting so prominent in migraine was a sympathetic interaction of the body with the head. The basis of his ideas was the humeral theory advanced by Hippocrates and the belief in the influence of the black bile on the brain.

The Talmud states that "an excess of blood is the main cause of all illnesses," a supposition which Galen later adhered to. The plethora or fullness of the blood vessels of the head was to be remedied by "a type of cedar (schurbina), tamarisk (bina), fresh myrtle and olive leaves, willow (chilpha), clove and other herbs." The instructions were: "Cook them together and take 300 for each side of the head." Another prescription was to "cook white roses with all the leaves on one side and take 60 cups thereof for each side of the head. Rose water,

---

[4] Quoted in: *The Headache Book*, by Arnold P. Friedman, Shervert H. Frazier, Jr., and Dodi Schultz (New York: Dodd, Mead, 1973).

either alone or with vinegar, was also recommended for head compresses."[5]

For a "partial pain" (or pain in half the head), the remedy prescribed was the slaughter of a white cock with a white zuz (or piece of money) "over that side of the patient which is painful (so that the blood flows on the head of the patient)." It was cautioned: "One must be careful with the blood in order not to blind the patient's eyes."[6] The slaughtered cock was then hung on the door post, and the patient rubbed his head against the bird upon entering and leaving the house.

In the Talmud, headache was the second most frequent ailment in the Orient, with only dysentery being more prevalent. When Jabez, in Chronicles I, prays that the Lord keep evil from him, it is a prayer for health, "that I not suffer from headache or earache or pain in the eyes." Rabbi Yochanan wore phylacteries on his head only in the winter "when his head was not heavy." Rabbi Judah of Siknin observed that if one twin sister had a headache, "the other felt it as well."[7]

Headaches due to wine consumption were known, particularly affecting those who could not hold liquor. Blowing into the foam of beverages, such as beer or mead, was called "damaging to the head." Rabbi Judah, after drinking the prescribed four cups of wine on Passover, had to bind his temples because of severe headache from Passover to Pentecost. He said: "One should not visit people suffering from headaches because speaking to them is harmful."[8]

Chronicles I states that the healthier physicians of antiquity recommended rubbing the head with wine, vinegar, or simply oil. The universal remedy for any ailment, including headache, was to occupy oneself with the words of God: "they are an ornament of grace unto thy head" (Proverbs 1:9).

[5] Preuss, *op. cit.*
[6] *Ibid.*
[7] *Ibid.*
[8] *Ibid.*

The status of migraine history and descriptions remained more or less unaltered until the early eighteenth century. In 1760, J. A. Van der Linden published a monograph which investigated the influence of ovarian activity on migraine. This monograph mentions many of the facts we now know about menstrual migraine. John Fordyce, in 1758, wrote about the association of facial shingles with migraine. In 1778, John Fothergill wrote a paper entitled "Remarks on That Complaint Known Under the Name of the Sick Headache."[9] In this paper he stated: "there is a disease which though it occurs very frequently, has not yet obtained a place in the systematic catalogues. It is commonly to be met with in practice, and is described by those who are affected with it, and who are not few in number, under the compound title of sick headache." He continued:

> Under this title they, at least, describe their feelings and, on a little inquiry, one finds that they are affected by both [nausea and headache]. This is not the complaint of any particular age, sex, constitution, or season, it is incident to all. The sedentary, relaxed, inactive and incautious respecting diet, are the most exposed to it; and who are yet, sometimes, not much less sufferers by the means frequently made use of to remove it, than by the disease itself.
>
> To collect into a short compass all the symptoms which accompany this disease would be difficult, and not so very interesting, to describe so many, as to make the complaint easy to be distinguished in the first place, and in what manner it may be treated with success, will be of more importance.
>
> Those who are affected with the sick headache most commonly describe it in this manner; that they awake in

[9] In: *The Works of John Fothergill, M.D.*, by John Coakley Lettsom (London: Charles Dilly), pp. 597–609.

the morning with a headache, which seldom affects the whole head, but one particular part of it, most commonly the forehead, over one frequently, sometimes above both eyes. Sometimes it is fixed about the upper part of the parietal bone, of one side only; sometimes and infrequently, the occiput is the part affected. Sometimes it darts from one to another of these places. It never goes entirely off, from the time it commences, till it wholly ceases, but is sometimes less tolerable.

With this is joined more or less of sickness, and which is just barely, in many people, not sufficient, without assistance, to provoke vomiting. If this pain does happen, as it most commonly comes on early in the morning, and before any meal is taken, seldom anything is thrown up but thin phlegm, unless the straining is severe, when some bitter or acid bile is brought up. In this case, the disease begins soon to abate, leaving a soreness about the head, a squeamishness at the stomach, and a general uneasiness, which induces the sick to wish for repose. Perhaps, after a short sleep, they recover perfectly well, only a little debilitated by their sufferings.[10]

By the mid-1860s, the malady went under the various names of Sick Headache, Fluid Headache, and Bilious Headache. The popular names recognized some of the most important features. But Edward Liveing believed that the vernacular term "megrim" was a medieval corruption of the Greek word "hemicrania," or half-headache. Dr. Liveing wrote a classic book in 1873, called *On Megrim, Sick Headache and Some Allied Disorders*. In this book, he spoke about the incurability of migraine. He believed that migraine was similar in nature to epilepsy, asthma, and neuralgia and the treatment for all of these diseases should be similar. He also noted that migraine was probably caused by a general mis-

[10] *Ibid.*

management of one's life or faulty habits, a feeling held today by many relatives of the migraineur. Liveing discussed his therapeutic objectives "to lessen the tendency of explosive action in the nervous centres by measures directed to the improvement of the general health, the removal of accessory causes and the direction of nervous energy into natural channels, as well as pharmaceutical remedies; and secondly, to avoid or remove the exciting of the seizures, and so to reduce as far as possible the number of attacks."[11] Liveing spoke about curing migraine through hygienic measures such as improvement in general health or correction of faulty hygienic conditions through improved diet, rest, and restorative remedies, and he also talked about pharmaceutical remedies such as sedatives, tonics, and specific drugs, none of which are used today to treat migraine.

Progress in the Twentieth Century

In the twentieth century, one of the greatest contributions to the understanding of headache was made by Harold G. Wolff and his Cornell University Group. They studied the effects of sterile inflammation present with migraine and described the physiology and pharmacology of many present-day treatments, such as ergotamine, in the aborting of migraine attacks. One of the most important facts they discovered was that in *all* migraine attacks there is an initial point when the blood vessels inside the head constrict or clamp down and then a secondary increase in size or swelling, a vasodilatation of the blood vessels, occurs both within and outside the skull. This is what causes the actual pain of the attack.

Dr. Wolff also demonstrated that, at the same time, an inflammation or sterile infection in the wall of the artery occurs

[11] Edward Liveing, *On Megrim, Sick Headache and Some Allied Disorders, a Contribution to the Pathology of Nerve-Storms* (London: J. & A. Churchill, 1873).

and that certain humeral substances are given off that produce and prolong the pain of headache. He showed that at the onset of an attack the blood chemical known as serotonin is greatly decreased. We know from Wolff's work that the warnings of migraine, the early neurological signs, the eye signs or the numbness in one arm or leg, result from this initial clamping down or vasoconstriction of the blood vessels.

We will discuss more recent theories of the possible causation of migraine when we talk about treatments of the future in Chapter 14.

Early Therapy for Headache

In 1700 B.C. some ancient writings referred to a remedy for headaches. This remedy consisted of the application of moist mortar to the head in an attempt to cool and thus relieve the affliction. Another early remedy was the combination of coriander, wormwood, juniper, honey, and opium. As early as the Neolithic Age, trepanning, or drilling holes in the head to allow the evil spirits to escape, was practiced to cure headaches. Trephining (skull boring) was a common operation in antiquity. Galen advised the taking of blood, or phlebotomy, and cold applications to the head as the treatment. Another ancient treatment was the application of a hot iron to the side of the headache or cutting a hole in the temple and applying garlic to this hole. Cups or leeches were used in the Middle Ages to treat headache. Counterirritants to a shaved head were another treatment. Galen advocated the use of an electric fish, called a torpedo, to the head, and it is interesting that today transcutaneous stimulation is used. It has been a help to some headache patients.

In 1883, in Germany, A. Eulenburg used injections of ergot extract, and later ergotamine, in five cases of headache, with some helpful results. In 1894, in the United States, W. H. Thomson suggested taking fluid extracts of ergot by mouth as soon as the early signs of migraine were noticed. He also talked about the rectal use of ergot to abort migraine.

Without doubt, the most important recent advance in the treatment of migraine has been the discovery of the effectiveness of propranolol in this disorder. The discovery was made by R. Rabkin and his associates in 1966, with a patient being treated with this drug for cardiac disease.[12] Its effectiveness was later confirmed in many clinical trials, and propranolol was approved as a prophylactic therapy for migraine by the Food and Drug Administration in 1979. To date, propranolol has remained a very effective and safe prophylactic agent for the person suffering from repeated migraine attacks.

[12] R. Rabkin et al., "The Prophylactic Value of Propranolol in Angina Pectoris," *American Journal of Cardiology*, 18:370–383 (1966).

3

TYPES OF HEADACHES

There are many different types of headaches, with different causes, different patterns, and different treatments and cures.

Normal Headaches

The common "tension" headache strikes almost everyone at some time in their life. This type of headache is not terribly serious and can usually be relieved by aspirin, acetaminophen (Tylenol), or other over-the-counter medications. It is not necessary for the infrequent "tension" headache sufferer to consult a physician. Tension headaches can be the result of stressful or pressure-filled situations. They can also be the result of poor posture—for instance, after excessive reading or a long car trip. At times exercise is helpful in relieving the headache symptom. In other instances, however, exertion may be detrimental to the headache problem.

Vascular Headaches

The term "vascular" refers to the "vessel carrying the blood," or "blood vessel." Vascular headache refers to a group of headache conditions in which blood vessel swelling is the major component in the production of pain. The blood vessels in the tissue surrounding the head swell and become distended, thus causing pain. Vascular headaches are usually throbbing in character, and physical exertion increases the pain. Included under the classification of vascular headaches are migraine headaches, cluster headaches, and toxic headaches. All involve vascular dilation, or a swelling of the blood vessels.

Migraine Headaches

Migraine headaches have been defined as a familial disorder characterized by recurrent attacks of headache. They vary in intensity, frequency, and duration. The headaches are usually unilateral, occurring on one side of the head, and are commonly associated with a loss of appetite, nausea, and vomiting. Some migraine headaches are associated with neurological and mood disturbances. The headache recurs at intervals, with complete freedom between attacks. A response to ergotamine tartrate is another criterion in making the diagnosis of migraine headache.

The headache phase may be preceded by a premonitory or warning sign called an aura. The aura is most often visual, but can involve sensory, motor, or speech impairments. It varies from person to person but usually remains fairly consistent for the individual. Only 20% of migraine sufferers have an aura preceding their headaches.

Migraine headaches have many symptoms, involving various parts of the body. These headaches are a configuration of symptoms that form a condition. An individual patient, however, may exhibit only some of the signs listed above.

Cluster Headaches

Cluster headaches are so named because the attacks group together, occurring one or more times daily, for several weeks or months, and then totally subside for periods of several months or even years. There is a tendency for the headache clusters to occur in the spring or autumn. The headache is one-sided and of short duration; it usually lasts from 15 minutes to two hours and may return at predictable times each day. The pain is very severe and of a burning quality. The location of the pain is most often behind or around the eye, and the eye on the affected side generally becomes red and often waters, with the eyelid drooping and the pupil constricting. The nostril on the affected side may become congested. Unlike migraine, there does not appear to be a familial tendency for cluster headaches.

Cluster Headache Variant

Recently the Diamond Headache Clinic reported a new headache syndrome. Actually, this syndrome is not new but was unrecognized for a number of years. The symptomatology of cluster headache variant, as it has been identified, is a combination of three separate types of headaches.

The first type is atypical cluster headache. These headaches are chronic and, like cluster headaches, occur several times a day. They are described as atypical because they do not always occur over the eye, they may last all day long, and they shift from one location to another. Second, these patients suffer from many short, jabbing or icepick-like pains in various locations throughout the head. Finally, the patients complain of a background vascular headache, typified by a chronic or continuous one-sided headache of variable severity, which is vascular due to its throbbing nature—it is very intense. Patients who exhibit at least two or three of these symptoms have been responsive to a drug used for arthritis, the anti-inflammatory agent indomethacin (Indocin). Fifty percent of the patients have obtained complete control of the headaches and 80% have experienced some relief with the use of indomethacin.

Toxic Headaches

Toxic headaches may be caused by fever, alcohol consumption, carbon dioxide retention, therapeutic or food substances containing nitrites or nitrates, and poisons. The most common nonmigrainous vascular headache is one produced by a fever accompanying such illnesses as influenza, mononucleosis, measles, mumps, pneumonia, tonsillitis, etc. The pain of the headache is similar to that of migraine. Medications to reduce the fever, such as aspirin, will also act on reducing the head pain. The typical hangover headache is also due to vasodilation of the blood vessels.

Any increase of carbon dioxide in the blood content or reduction in oxygen results in extreme cerebral vasodilation. Consumption of or exposure to nitrates and nitrites causes vasodilation of blood vessels and, thus, vascular headaches. Nitrates are found in medications for heart problems and in chemicals used in the munitions industry. Nitrites are used as preservatives in curing certain processed meats. Monosodium glutamate is another food substance that produces vascular-type headaches. Withdrawal from caffeine, such as missing the morning cup of coffee, and various other drugs, also can cause vasodilation. Poisons, such as lead, benzene, carbon tetrachloride, and insecticides, can in themselves produce vascular headaches.

Organic Causes

Headaches brought on entirely by organic causes are traction headaches or inflammatory headaches. They are signs that something is physically amiss with the body or, most often, the head. These headaches may be symptoms of any number of problems, including disorders of the sinuses, teeth, eyes, neck, and brain. Treatment for headaches with organic causes must involve treatment of the specific underlying problem.

Sinuses

Case History 1

N.S., aged 22, has headaches which started two weeks before her first visit. The pain is bifrontal, above the bridge of the nose, and occurs daily. The headaches last three to four hours. They begin gradually in the morning and increase in severity throughout the day. The pain is moderate to severe and pressure-like. Her nose feels congested, and there is discharge from both nostrils. Since the onset of the headaches, N.S. has had an intermittent fever. The patient denies any anxiety or depression, and there is no family history of headaches. The headaches are not seasonally related. Her medical and surgical histories are negative. The patient notes that the headaches do not increase with food or alcohol.

When a sinus becomes inflamed, it can cause localized head pain. Allergic reactions and tumors in the sinuses can also produce inflammation, swelling, and blockage of the sinuses. However, vascular headaches can cause similar symptoms. The vast majority of people who think they are experiencing "sinus" problems are actually suffering from a vascular type of headache. When sinus disease is the cause of the headache, an accompanying fever is often present, and x-rays will indicate some sinus blockage. One or both nostrils are blocked and the pain extends over the cheek or forehead. The area is tender to the touch.

The sinuses are found in the forehead bone, the cheek bone on each side, and behind the bridge of the nose. The sinuses are filled with air, and their secretions must be able to drain freely into the nose. Treatment of sinus problems often involves antibiotics for the infection, as well as antihistamines and powerful decongestants. Draining of the sinuses is occasionally necessary. Surgical corrections are usually not indicated, nor have they been found to be beneficial.

Teeth

Poor dental alignment, gum infections, and arthritis of the jaw can cause head pain. Jaw clenching and teeth gnashing can also cause headaches. Pain may be felt in the temples, in the ear region, or radiating down the neck to the shoulders. Normally, the opposing teeth interlock during chewing and swallowing. A dental malocclusion exists if the interjaw relationship is disturbed. Clicking of the jaw may indicate a faulty bite. With natural teeth, head and face pain caused by malocclusions may occur on either one or both sides. The pain usually begins on awakening and occurs in people who grind their teeth. Teeth grinding often reflects tension. There are abnormal jaw movements in grinding the teeth that are triggered by dental malocclusions. Most headaches of this type arise in people with faulty dentures or in those who have had teeth extracted. A dull ache is felt in both temples and stretches across the forehead. The pain can begin at any time of the day and last for several hours.

Eyes

Pain caused by eye disturbances can be referred to other areas of the head, while pain from other areas can be felt in the eye region. Many headache problems that have other foundations are blamed on "eyestrain." Eyestrain indicates that the person needs glasses or has an imbalance in the eye muscles so that considerable effort is required on the part of the eye muscles to keep the eyes aligned. This added muscular activity can cause head pain, but not to the extent that is commonly believed. Headaches due to eyestrain are most often located around the eyes and forehead. A change in eyeglasses, better lighting conditions, and discontinuing reading or close work will probably offer relief of the headache. Eye exercises may also help. Usually, however, a closer look into the cause of the headache is needed.

Glaucoma is a disease of the eyes that can cause headaches. The fluid from the eyes does not drain properly, or there is overproduction of fluid, which causes pressure within the eye. This increased pressure can lead to blindness if not corrected. The headache caused by glaucoma may be felt in the region of one or both eyes or the forehead and may be mild or severe in intensity. Nausea and vomiting may accompany the headache. Some forms of glaucoma may be mistaken for migraine due to the similar symptoms. A correct diagnosis can be made by measuring the pressure in the eyeball. People suffering from glaucoma may experience a fogging of vision or see colored halos around objects. Many drugs, including certain over-the-counter medications such as antihistamines, can worsen the condition of glaucoma and must be avoided. Prompt medical attention is necessary. Infrequently, eye infections and tumors of the eye can also cause headaches.

Ears

Diseases involving the ear may result in headaches in the temple region, while disorders of the nose, throat, and teeth can refer the head pain to the ear area. The correct source of the headache must be determined and the organic problem treated; in this way, the headache problem will be alleviated.

Neck

Neck disorders may cause or accompany headaches, as nerve fibers overlap. Any pain extending over the back of the head could stem from a neck problem. A whiplash injury or rheumatoid arthritis usually affects the upper neck and refers pain to the back of the head. An injured person holds his neck in an abnormal position, resulting in strain on the neck muscles.

Another head pain arising from the upper neck and caused by poor neck posture is a pain shooting to the eye and forehead. A muscle contraction headache can occur as the result of a stiff neck, and pain may be felt in the back of the head as well as the neck. Scalp muscles can also be involved, producing a more generalized headache. Headaches arising from neck problems may respond to traction (such as the wearing of a cervical collar), neck manipulation, heat, or a local anesthetic.

Brain

Case History 2

T.E., aged 65, began to note difficulty with his vision. He stated that his vision to the right was impaired. He found it difficult to read. He was bumping into objects on the right side of his environment. He consulted an ophthalmologist, who performed visual fields and elicited a field defect, although the patient's cooperation was not optimal.

T.E. had a long history of chronic frontal and temporal headaches, which he associated with hay fever and sinusitis. He stated that these headaches had not increased, but during the course of the interview and examination he admitted that he had more pain on the left side of the head, which was relatively constant and not easily relieved by medications. He described great turmoil recently, associated with problems with the IRS. These business difficulties had been trying, and he blamed many of his current complaints on them. He was taking large quantities of medication, including a sleeping pill, a tranquilizer, and an antihistamine, and he used cigarettes and alcohol liberally.

When examined, he showed a significant loss of visual acuity, with a definite visual field cut on the right. His recent memory was poor. His speech was slow and suggested sedation. There was minimal weakness of the right leg. The patient followed directions poorly and seemed confused.

He was admitted to a hospital, where appropriate studies were done, and a mass lesion was found in the left temporal and occipital area of the brain. He was transferred to a neurosurgical facility, where a well-circumscribed and encapsulated tumor was removed.

The brain itself is not sensitive to pain. Thus, diseases of the brain cause pain only when they displace blood vessels, block the flow of cerebrospinal fluid, or irritate the meninges. The fear of a brain tumor is prominent in the thinking of most headache sufferers. However, very few headaches are caused by brain tumors, and not all people with brain tumors experience headaches. A traction type of headache is a symptom of a brain tumor. A tumor will cause headaches if it places arteries under tension by infringing on their space or increases intracranial pressure in some other way. The location of the tumor will determine the timing of the headache symptoms. Headaches associated with a tumor have a sudden and recent onset and most often do not appear until late in the course of the tumor, usually after other neurological symptoms have been noted. If a tumor is the cause of the headache, there are usually other symptoms indicative of the tumor, with the headache pain usually intermittent and not very severe. Vascular headaches and headaches caused by neuralgias are often of greater intensity. The headache of a tumor may be felt over the entire head or only in a localized area of the head. The headache gets progressively worse and is intensified by coughing or sudden movements of the head. However, this can be true of other types of headaches as well, such as "exertional" headaches. A tumor may be benign or malignant. Many can be surgically removed completely, without any further problems.

An increase in intracranial pressure also causes headaches by placing the arteries under tension. Any blockage of the flow of the cerebrospinal fluid would increase intracranial pressure. Such headaches are intensified by bending the head forward. The fluid surrounding the brain must maintain a certain pressure or a headache will result. Such a headache is often the result of a lumbar puncture, a test done by withdrawing a small amount of cerebrospinal fluid from the lower back. The use of a small gauge needle during the procedure helps to prevent a headache problem. The dull, deep, throbbing headache is usually best remedied by lying flat in bed for a few days following the test.

Meningitis, an inflammation of the meninges, the tissue covering the brain, can cause a severe headache with stiffness of the neck. There is usually an accompanying high fever, rapid pulse, and sweating, as in other infections. Photophobia, a sensitivity to light, may also be present. The headache generally lasts a few days. Encephalitis, an inflammation of the brain itself, causes headaches since the meninges are involved in the inflammation.

Case History 3

J.B., a 33-year-old man, was in his usual state of good health. He maintained his weight at moderate levels and was abstemious in his habits. A recent complete physical examination had been within normal limits. He had never complained of headache.

Two weeks ago, while jogging, he experienced a sudden and severe head pain involving his entire head; the pain did not wax and wane and was not relieved by rest. He became ill and vomited, and found no relief from aspirin, codeine, or an ice pack applied to his head. Shortly thereafter he became sleepy and was not easily roused. His wife recognized immediately that a serious illness had occurred, and brought him to the emergency room of a nearby hospital. He could not walk from the car to the examining room.

On admission, he was restless and moaning in pain, and could not give an adequate history. One pupil had become dilated, but other signs of neurological damage were not prominent. He was not paralyzed and had developed only slight stiffness of the neck. A spinal tap was done within the hour, and the spinal fluid obtained was bloody. After consultation among several specialists, angiograms were performed; they showed a leaking aneurysm in one of the brain arteries.

A sudden, intense headache can be caused by irritation of the meninges by blood spilled into the subarachnoid space from a ruptured blood vessel. This is the space between the innermost covering of the brain and the brain itself. A subarachnoid hemorrhage is almost always accompanied by headache. The headache comes on suddenly and is very severe. The pain begins in the head and radiates down the neck and back. It is often accompanied by vomiting, drowsiness, a stiff neck, and loss of consciousness. A subdural hemorrhage is usually accompanied by headache, the headache being mild, generalized, and fairly constant, but gradually increasing in intensity. Other neurological symptoms appear as the hemorrhage displaces pain-sensitive blood vessels. A subdural hemorrhage is usually caused by a head injury. A head injury can also cause an epidural hemorrhage by rupturing the meninges of the brain. This headache is severe and comes on suddenly, leading rapidly to mental confusion and a comatose state.

Following a head injury, there are different types of headache, depending on the damaged area. There is no consistent relationship between the severity of the headache and the severity of the injury. If an artery is injured, short bursts of localized headache may occur. If a vein is damaged, pain may follow only after exertion. When a nerve is affected, pain will occur in the sharply defined area of the pinched nerve. Any headache that results from a head injury demands prompt medical care. Headaches can occur after a concussion—a loss of consciousness, usually brief, which most often occurs after a blow to the head. Headaches due to a concussion will usually diminish with the passage of time.

An aneurysm can also cause head pain. An aneurysm is a bulging out of a blood vessel, similar to a small balloon. It suddenly appears in the brain in a weak spot in the wall of a blood vessel. The symptoms are similar to those of migraine headaches—a very intense, regular, throbbing pain that appears first in the forehead or behind one or both eyes. The headache must be treated by cooling down the aneurysm with complete rest, and then tying it off surgically before it ruptures. Headache can also be a symptom of an impending stroke (a cerebrovascular accident) due to a blocked blood vessel in the brain; or a headache can appear following a stroke. Headaches can also herald a cerebral embolism.

Muscle Contraction (Tension) Headaches

The most common kind of headache is the muscle contraction (tension) headache. It comprises 85% to 90% of the headache problems seen by physicians. The pain in muscle contraction headache is usually described as diffuse and surrounding the head, as a tightness or band around the head (the "hatband effect"), or as a pinched feeling in the muscles of the neck. There is often a dull aching in the forehead. The temples, the back of the head, or the jaw may also be involved. The muscle contraction headache may be described more as a constant feeling of pressure than as pain. Ninety percent of these headaches affect both sides of the head. Often, jabs of sharp pain are felt through the dull ache. The headache is usually persistent and localized in one area, while the intensity varies throughout the day for weeks, months, or years. Muscle contraction headaches usually strike often, although they vary a great deal in duration and frequency. One person may experience a headache for one or two hours once a week, while another person may suffer every day for years, with the headache never relenting.

The pain originates with the constant contraction of the jaw, face, scalp, and neck muscles. The contraction of the muscles can often be felt by touching them, and they may be tender to the touch. The muscles feel normal between headaches. The major scalp arteries tend to constrict during muscle contraction headaches. The pain is intensified by ergotamine tartrate, which constricts the blood vessels. This is in contrast to ergotamine tartrate relieving the pain in vascular headaches. In muscle contraction headaches, the pain is often relieved by alcohol, which causes the blood vessels to dilate. This is unlike other types of headaches, where alcohol intensifies or brings on a headache.

Mental tension is associated with muscle tension. Stress can cause the individual to tighten his muscles, and the taut muscles can cause pain. In many instances, however, emotional stress is not present. A majority of muscle contraction headache patients suffer from depression. The depression is not a "feeling blue" sensation, but a serious and lengthy depression, lasting even years. The muscle contraction headache may also be a sign of chronic anxiety. Those headaches caused by anxiety come on unpredictably, at almost any time, while depression headaches establish a regular pattern, usually occurring in the early morning and early evening. A sleep disturbance invariably accompanies the muscle contraction headache. The headaches themselves are not usually of an intensity to awaken a person; however, the accompanying depression or anxiety causes sleep problems. Those patients with headaches related to anxiety have difficulty falling asleep, while those with depression usually awaken early in the morning or frequently, throughout the night. Other characteristics of the muscle contraction headache include a lack of response to simple analgesics, an increase in the severity of the headache in the mornings, and an increase in headaches on weekends and holidays. Muscle contraction headaches are familial only in the respect of "learned" behavior. There are none of the accompanying neurological symptoms found with other types of headaches.

Special Types of Headaches

The following types of headaches are caused by very specific agents or circumstances. It is necessary to identify the "trigger," or precipitating factor, in the headache. Many of these triggers can be avoided, thus leading to simple control of the headache problem.

Hot Dog Headache

Foods containing sodium nitrite can cause headaches in people with a sensitivity to it. Sodium nitrite is contained in many preserved foods such as hot dogs, sausages, salami, ham, bacon, and other cured meat products. Nitrite added to salt gives meat a uniform red appearance. People employed in munitions plants can suffer similar headaches if they are sensitive to nitrate compounds. Dynamite, for instance, contains nitrates, which can be absorbed through the skin, thus causing the headaches. Tolerance for nitrates will sometimes develop after prolonged use. Headaches of this type are also found in people taking medications for coronary heart disease, such as nitroglycerin. The headache is a vascular type of headache and appears to affect migrainous persons. It is dull and aching and may be associated with a flushing of the face. The headaches are similar to migraine except in pattern. Avoiding foods with nitrites and medications containing nitrates, and

avoiding exposure to these substances, will alleviate the headache problem in those sensitive to these vasoactive substances.

Ice Cream Headache

A severe, brief, frontal headache can occur after eating
ice cream. It can actually happen when any cold substance is
applied to the roof of the mouth. The pain is usually dull and
throbbing. It can be felt in the face, throat, or head, and often
radiates all over the head, as the fifth cranial nerve carries the
sensation from the front of the mouth and refers it along its
many branches. The pain lasts for only a few minutes. The
head pain may be helped by slowly cooling the mouth with
small amounts of the cold substance. People who suffer from
migraine and cluster headaches are especially prone to the ice
cream headache.

Fasting Headache

Lack of food can cause headaches. Skipping a meal or
lowering the blood sugar level may trigger a migraine headache. A dull pain characterizes the "fasting" headache. A
person who tends to get early morning headaches or headaches
after dieting may be a victim of the fasting headache, although
it must be noted that not all early morning headaches are caused
by low blood sugar. A fasting headache does not necessarily
mean that one has hypoglycemia or low blood sugar. A person
can develop a headache merely from a drop in the blood sugar
level. This type of headache can often be prevented by con-
suming a high-protein snack before bed or between meals to
keep the blood sugar at a constant level. Protein digests slowly,
while carbohydrates are burned up quickly. Once the headache
has begun, however, eating will have little effect. Fasting
headaches can often be prevented by making certain that meals
are not delayed or skipped. The "weekend" headache is also
often caused by a drop in blood sugar. A person tends to sleep

later on Saturday or Sunday mornings, thus throwing off the blood sugar balance in the body.

Caffeine Withdrawal Headache

Caffeine is contained in coffee, tea, colas, and chocolate, and is also a component of many headache medications such as Empirin, Excedrin, Anacin, Darvon Compound, Vanquish, Norgesic, Cafergot, and Fiorinal. With continual intake of any of these substances, the blood vessels may adapt to a semi-constricted state since caffeine constricts the blood vessels. Withdrawal from caffeine can then cause head pain. A sudden wearing off of the effect of caffeine can lead to abrupt vaso-dilation and a "caffeine withdrawal" headache. Caffeine is also a stimulant, which can add a letdown feeling after the effect wears off.

This kind of headache is common in heavy coffee drink-ers. One of the factors contributing to "weekend" or "holi-day" headaches may be caffeine withdrawal. If a person normally consumes large amounts of caffeine-containing sub-stances during the week, a withdrawal, rebound headache may result on weekends or holidays if similar amounts are not consumed. The pain-producing mechanism of the headache is the vasodilation of cranial arteries. The headache may be a persistent, generalized one that lasts for weeks. A gradual withdrawal from caffeine-containing substances can help to bring these headaches under control.

Drug-Induced Headache

Case History 4

W. F., aged 61, notes that his headaches started five years previously. He had a history of one-sided headaches until the age of 50. The current headaches are located in the occipital area and above the right and left eyes. They occur daily, lasting four to six hours. The head pain is sharp, severe, and steady, sometimes localized to one side of the head. The headaches awaken the patient at night. There is no family history of headaches. The patient's medical history reveals hypertension, and he has had a cholecystectomy. The patient has not noticed an increase in headaches with certain foods or alcoholic beverages. He is currently on Serpasil 0.25 mg, four times daily, and has been taking this for the past five years. (Serpasil contains reserpine, a drug discovered in India which helps high blood pressure.) He is not on any prophylactic headache medications.

Many medications can themselves cause head pain. Nitroglycerin or amyl nitrate is often given to heart patients whose coronary arteries have narrowed and cause pain, or to patients with circulatory problems due to a hardening of the arteries. These medications deliberately cause the dilation of blood vessels to ease the coronary or arterial problems but may provoke a throbbing headache as a side-effect. Patients with arthritis or other joint and muscle pain are often treated effectively with indomethacin, which can provoke a continuous, dull headache in some people. Indomethacin produces a chemical vasodilation. Medications that are used in the treatment of epilepsy and high blood pressure, such as reserpine, hydralazine, and some diuretics, can also cause headaches. Certain antidepressants such as monoamine oxidase inhibitors, while used as a worthwhile treatment for many headache sufferers, can actually cause headaches in others. In addition, some amphetamines and decongestants can bring on headache symptoms in some people.

The use of female hormones by menopausal women or birth control pills will dramatically add to the headache problem in migraine-prone women. Headaches can become more frequent, of greater intensity, and of longer duration as a result of such hormonal medications. This topic will be dealt with in greater detail in the chapter on migraine headaches.

Withdrawal from many medications can also provoke headaches. As mentioned in the previous section, the headache sufferer who continually takes caffeine-containing analgesic preparations may experience a rebound type of headache upon withdrawal of the medication. A similar situation results from the drug ergotamine. Taking ergotamine every day for two to four consecutive days in order to prevent a vascular headache will instead provoke such a headache. This is called a rebound headache. The use of nicotine can cause a similar cycle with resulting headaches.

Exertional Headache

An exertional headache is transient and accompanies or follows such activities as running, lifting, bending, coughing, sneezing, or straining with a bowel movement. For those susceptible to exertional headaches, almost any type of exercise or limited exertion can provoke the headache. The onset is sudden and directly related to the activity. The pain is of short duration, from a few seconds to a few minutes. Exertional headaches may be caused by blood vessel changes or the depletion of certain biological substances in the body. During exercise one's blood pressure and pulse rate are elevated, and thus the arteries dilate. Any type of treatment aimed at constricting the cerebral blood vessels before exertion may be helpful in preventing this type of headache. A sweetened drink before or during exercise may help to avoid the headache. Muscles may be using their stored glycogen during exertion. However, the need for glucose is not the only factor involved. Exertional headaches must be closely monitored as they may be associated with organic disease such as a brain lesion. Fortunately, the benign forms of exertional headaches are far more common than those with organic causes.

Cough Headache

The "cough" headache is a form of exertional headache. It is a vascular type of headache that may occur during or directly after a coughing spell. The pain is of short duration, sometimes lasting only seconds, and is usually felt on both sides of the head. Someone suffering from a cough headache should seek medical attention as it could be a sign of an obstruction in the brain fluids (cerebrospinal fluid). There are "benign" cough headaches, however, which exist with no tumor or other abnormality.

Monosodium Glutamate Headache

Monosodium glutamate is a seasoning and a flavor enhancer, and is used as a preservative in many foods. It can produce a generalized vasomotor reaction, which may include headache. In sensitive individuals, very small quantities can cause a burning sensation in the face, sweating, a feeling of pressure or tightness in the chest, as well as a headache. The symptoms occur about 20 minutes after a meal and last for approximately one hour. The headache is felt as pressure or a pounding pain over the temples and a tight bandlike sensation around the forehead. The symptoms are the result of monosodium glutamate acting directly on the blood vessels. It affects the chemicals around the brain that cause the blood vessels to swell. Many people who suffer from monosodium glutamate headaches are also afflicted with other vascular headaches such as migraine.

The group of symptoms associated with this headache is referred to as the "Chinese restaurant syndrome" since monosodium glutamate is used extensively as a flavor enhancer in Chinese food, especially wonton soup. Wonton soup contains large amounts of monosodium glutamate and is usually the first course in a Chinese meal. Those people sensitive to monosodium glutamate should avoid eating foods that have been treated with it, especially on an empty stomach, as an empty stomach greatly increases the possibility of the syndrome occurring. The presence of other food in the stomach seems to deaden or block the effects of monosodium glutamate.

It is estimated that up to one-quarter of the population may have a sensitivity to this preservative. As just noted, if a person has determined that he is susceptible to this type of headache, it is best to eliminate foods containing monosodium glutamate from the diet. Monosodium glutamate can be found as an ingredient in many instant and canned soups, processed meats, frozen dinners, seasonings, and meat tenderizers, as well as in Chinese food.

Tartrazine is an orange-yellow powder used as a coloring agent for medicines and certain foods. It, too, can cause headaches in people with a predisposition toward migraine.

Sexual Headache

Case History 5

R.A., a 42-year-old man who is a perfectionist and has a compulsive personality, came into the office complaining of two kinds of headaches. One started at the age of 15; it was unilateral and occurred once or twice a month, with a duration of one to two days. The headache was severe, and the patient had a history of seeing jagged lines in one eye before many of the headaches started. He also had severe nausea, vomiting, and some photosensitivity with the headache. His father had had similar headaches. The headaches were not seasonally related, and there was no allergic association. He had had numerous workups for this type of headache since he was a youngster, and a diagnosis of migraine had been made. He was able to abort the headaches with the use of ergotamine tartrate and caffeine tablets. Usually, about four tablets were required. He was successfully treated on this regimen.

The second type of headache started about six months before his visit and had its first occurrence during sexual excitement. He had had five such episodes of headache associated with sexual intercourse. However, the headache did not occur with all episodes of intercourse and seemed to develop slowly during sexual activity, reaching its greatest intensity at the moment of orgasm. The headache was located occipitally, in contrast to the migraine, which was frontal in most instances. The sex headache was bilateral and involved his neck and radiated forward to both sides of the parietal region. The patient described the pain as dull, cramping in quality, but on two occasions it had been throbbing and severe, although not as excruciating as his migraine attacks. There was no nausea, vomiting, or aura connected with this headache. The headache was related to a degree of sexual excitement, and it took almost seven hours for it to subside. He noticed that his heart was beating fast and he had throbbing in the ears and a flushed facial feeling associated with this headache problem. The patient had a complete neurological examination, and the findings were normal. Because of the exertional nature of the headache, a CAT scan with infusion was performed, and was completely normal.

Headaches can be associated with sexual activity, especially with orgasm. There are two types of these headaches. In the first type, the excitement accompanying intercourse causes muscle contraction in the head and neck, thus leading to head pain. The second type is a vascular headache. It is a very intense, severe headache usually occurring just before orgasm. It has been called an "orgasmic headache," or "orgasmic cephalalgia." In some instances, the headache is a response to an increase in blood pressure, in which the blood vessels dilate. The headache is not usually related to the amount of physical exertion involved in intercourse. The pain may be located around or behind the eyes. It can last for hours or just a few minutes. The headache is made worse by movement. The headache may be a "benign" orgasmic headache; however, the possibility of organic disease should be thoroughly investigated. An orgasmic headache could be a symptom of a brain hemorrhage (bleeding around or inside the brain), stroke, or tumor. An accompanying stiffness in the neck is often an indication of bleeding into the spinal fluid. The benign orgasmic headache occurs more frequently in men than women and usually strikes migraine sufferers. Benign orgasmic headache is often effectively treated with migraine medications, blood-vessel-constricting agents, taken before intercourse.

Headache Due to the Facial Neuralgias

Case History 6

I.A., aged 60, has complained of headache since age 54. The pain is unilateral, directly below the right cheekbone, and severe, jabbing, lasting 15 to 30 seconds, with periods of abatement of about one hour. The groups of attacks last approximately one hour. This has been continuing on and off for about six years. The patient complains of attacks occurring when cold air hits her face. Cold drinks can increase attacks, and chewing can also bring them on. There is occasional tearing of the right eye. The patient notes that she has more attacks during the winter. She also notes that food and alcohol do not increase the headaches. The medical and surgical histories are noncontributory, nor is there any family history of headache.

Neuralgia is a term used to refer to persistent pain in the face and head. The pain arises from an abnormality in a nerve or its connections. The major neuralgias are trigeminal neuralgia and glossopharyngeal neuralgia. Trigeminal neuralgia is a rare condition and refers to any pain originating from the trigeminal nerve (the fifth cranial nerve), which is responsible for sensations in the face and front part of the scalp. Trigeminal neuralgia, also called tic douloureux, usually occurs in elderly people and affects women more frequently than men. The pain of trigeminal neuralgia is one of the most severe head pains. It is one-sided and of a very intense burning or jabbing quality. The pain is of short duration, lasting 20 to 30 seconds, often followed by a short relief period, which is then followed by another painful jab, repeating the cycle over and over again. The attacks generally last for an hour or longer and may be followed by an aching pain. These episodes may continue for weeks or months. The symptoms may then go into remission for months or even years.

Trigeminal neuralgia is associated with an increased sensitivity in the areas of the face supplied by the trigeminal nerve. People suffering from trigeminal neuralgia avoid activities that would involve irritating the sensitive "trigger zones" that produce pain. Activities such as chewing, talking, laughing, shaving, washing, or even a small gust of wind hitting the face can cause excruciating pain. Thus, trigeminal neuralgia sufferers may have a rather unkempt appearance. Anticonvulsant drugs can help to reduce the sensitivity of the "trigger zones" and relieve the pain, although many people suffering from trigeminal neuralgia may require neurological surgery.

Glossopharyngeal neuralgia affects the nerve that supplies sensation to the back of the tongue, the throat, and the ear. It has a jabbing type of pain, which is felt in the ear and back of the throat on one side. The pain may be brought on by yawning, swallowing, eating, coughing, or talking. Anticonvulsant medications have again been found to offer some relief. As migraine headache patients grow older, the character of their headaches may change. The migraine headaches may take on the form of episodic neuralgic pain affecting the ear or cheek unilaterally.

Atypical facial neuralgia refers to those painful conditions without "trigger zones." The pain is of a steady, diffuse, or aching quality, lasting hours or days. The pain may be felt in the area of the cheek, nose, and upper gum. It fluctuates in intensity and is greatly influenced by the patient's mood. It is a difficult condition to treat, as the origin of the pain is not known. Some people with atypical facial pain, especially of a throbbing nature, may be suffering from a kind of migraine or vascular headache.

Hypertensive Headache

Case History 7

D.S., 47 years old, has headaches that started one year before his visit. The pain is bilateral, affecting the right and left temples, top of the head, and frontal area. The headaches occur daily, starting in the morning but gradually diminishing as the day progresses. The headache can last from two to three hours to all day. The pain is pounding, varying from moderate to severe, and increases when the patient stoops, coughs, or exercises. The patient complains of anxiousness and nervousness but denies depression or family problems. He states that he does have some job pressures. His sleep pattern is not affected, but he occasionally wakes up with a severe headache in the morning. There is no family history of headache. The medical history reveals that the patient is hypertensive and obese. His surgical history is negative.

A hypertensive headache is caused by elevated blood pressure. Contrary to popular belief, most people who suffer from high blood pressure do not suffer from headaches. A headache is rarely provoked by mildly or moderately elevated blood pressure. People with more severe degrees of hypertension more often experience headaches as an accompanying symptom.

The headache associated with hypertension is vascular in nature, and the severity of the headache is related to the degree of hypertension. This headache more often affects older people. It is usually felt in the back of the head and neck, with the pain intensified by movement and having a dull, pounding, aching quality. The hypertensive headache occurs most often upon awakening and gradually disappears as the day progresses. Elevation of the head during sleep may be of some benefit.

Hypertension can increase the frequency of migraine headaches. People suffering from migraine headaches are considered more likely to develop high blood pressure. Unfortunately, many of the drugs used to treat hypertension, such as reserpine, hydralazine, and certain diuretics, can themselves provoke headaches. Efforts to control the hypertensive headache must involve efforts to bring the blood pressure to within normal limits. Lowering the blood pressure will help decrease the frequency and severity of the accompanying headaches. Loss of weight, a decrease in salt intake, and relaxation may be of help in lowering the blood pressure.

There are also headaches associated with sudden increases in blood pressure, such as those occurring in extreme emotional states or with exercise. These headaches are usually pounding and occur on both sides of the head. They are transient, and most often do not require any specific treatment.

Hypoglycemic Headache

The hypoglycemic headache is caused by low blood sugar. Reducing the sugar content of the blood causes cerebral vasodilation, and thus vascular headaches, especially migraine, can be triggered. There is a link between migraine headaches and blood sugar level. It is interesting to note that in instances when blood sugar levels are high, such as the onset of diabetes, pregnancy, and periods of weight gain, migraine attacks decrease in frequency and severity.

The headache associated with low blood sugar is dull and throbbing and is often accompanied by faintness and giddiness. The headaches often begin in the early morning. A protein snack before bed may counteract these headaches, as protein can be digested slowly throughout the night. Hypoglycemic headaches often can be avoided by eating regularly or eating small meals that are well spaced throughout the day. Also, avoiding foods that lead to a rapid rise and fall of the blood sugar level, such as carbohydrates, can help in controlling the headache problem. A snack before or after strenuous activity is also recommended. Oversleeping should be avoided since the body's normal blood sugar level is altered by excessive sleep.

Endocrine Gland Dysfunction and Headache

The endocrine glands include the thyroid gland, the adrenal glands, the gonads, the pancreas, the pituitary gland, and the parathyroid glands. They secrete hormones into the bloodstream. If any of the glands are not functioning properly, for a wide variety of reasons, many symptoms can appear, with headache among them. One example is hypothyroidism, in which there is a lack of thyroxin, a substance secreted by the thyroid gland. The accompanying headache may be recurring and severe, without an established pattern or location. Other symptoms include rapid weight gain and a general feeling of fatigue. Replacement of the necessary hormone is usually the recommended treatment. It is necessary to find the actual cause of any headache caused by a glandular malfunction and treat it appropriately, rather than just treating the headache symptom.

Carotidynia

Carotidynia involves an increase in the size and the beating of the carotid artery. This is the large artery that brings circulation to the head. If it becomes relaxed and distended, it will cause severe pain in the neck. The carotid artery may throb and feel tender. Carotidynia is closely related to vascular headaches, particularly migraine. It occurs more frequently in women and older people. Medications used in the treatment of migraine headaches are generally found to be effective in carotodynia.

4

HEADACHE HISTORY:
A KEY TO YOUR PROBLEM

It is not uncommon for a doctor to prescribe a pain-relieving medication for a headache problem without completing a thorough history, physical exam, and neurological examination. Many patients have undergone exhaustive testing, including tests with considerable risks and dangers, while adequate histories of their problems were not completed. The key to the diagnosis of any headache problem is a careful and thorough history. Frequently, the physical, neurological, and laboratory examinations are completely normal in their findings, and the only diagnostic basis is an accurate recording of the events and character of the headache problem.

Type of Headache

At the Diamond Headache Clinic one of the first questions asked of a patient is: "How many types of headaches do you have?" People with mixed headache problems—such as, migraine with muscle contraction headache—are frequently seen. Some patients complain of as many as four separate headache problems.

Mode of Onset

The manner in which the headache first begins is very important. Sudden onset of a headache would alert the physician to the possibility of an organic cause. A person with a long history of headaches which have not changed in character would be considered to have a chronic problem. Severe, sudden onset of headache accompanied by other symptoms, such as paralysis, weakness, or sensory disturbances such as pinprick sensations, might signify a cerebral hemorrhage. If a person has recurrent headaches with symptom-free intervals, this would suggest a vascular headache such as migraine or cluster headache.

In determining the mode of onset of the headache, we are also interested in the length of time the patient has had headaches. Many patients with migraine or depression will give 20-, 30-, or 40-year histories of headache. An extensive history of headaches indicates that we are probably not dealing with a serious organic disease.

Of particular interest is the age at which the headaches start. If the headaches begin before the age of 40, they are usually migraine. However, if the headaches start later in life, one should always be suspicious of organic pathology or psychological illness such as depression. Headache onset following a surgical procedure, childbirth, death of a loved one, or a serious economic loss may alert the physician to an underlying depression. Acute sinus headache usually starts gradually in the morning and increases in intensity as the day progresses. However, headaches due to high blood pressure are worse upon awakening and often disappear as the day continues. The headache that rouses a person in the middle of the night is most often a cluster-type headache. Many patients will wake up with a migraine present, but rarely will a migraine be severe enough to cause early waking.

Location

The location of head pain is frequently misleading and may not indicate the presence of an underlying disease. Vascular headaches, such as migraine or cluster headaches, are usually unilateral. It is also important to determine if the pain switches sides, as migraine frequently acts in this manner while cluster headache remains on the same side. Head pain that is generalized or in a hat-band distribution may indicate a psychological factor. Previously, organic disease was suspected if the headache persisted on one side, but this is not always true and is often misunderstood by neurologists.

Timing

Migraine headache is an intermittent disorder occurring at different intervals, with various symptom-free periods. In contrast, muscle contraction headache is usually constant and may continue for months, weeks, or years. These patients frequently note an increase in pain intensity with activity. A simple tension or muscle contraction headache due to anxiety may be constant, or it may appear at any time of day. However, if underlying depression is present, there is a diurnal variation, that is, the pain is worse in the morning and late afternoon.

Frequency

Migraine may occur at sporadic intervals during a lifetime. Eventually, medical advice is sought and an identifiable pattern is established, such as an association with menstruation. Migraine patients may be headache-free after the third month of pregnancy. During a vacation, patients may be headache-free, but there are also patients who will get headaches during periods of relaxation. Cluster headache is seasonal and most often occurs in spring and fall. The clusters occur in limited cycles, although some patients will have chronic cluster headaches.

Duration

If the headache is due to an organic cause such as a brain tumor, it is usually constant and continuous and will progressively increase in intensity. Migraine occurs periodically and can last anywhere from six hours to seven days, or longer. Cluster head pain can last from several minutes to almost four hours. Muscle contraction headache is usually persistent.

Severity of Pain

The pain of migraine is often described as intense, pulsating, or throbbing and not as a constant pain. This is due to the vascular nature of the disease. Cluster headache also is throbbing, but it is frequently described as a deep, boring, and severe, unbearable pain. With tic douloureux, or facial neuralgia, the pain is shocklike, transient, or stabbing. It is typically neuritic in character. The pain of muscle contraction headache is often dull, nagging, and persistent, with exacerbations appearing during the day, primarily in the early morning and late afternoon.

Warning Signs

Warnings are most common with migraine and usually are limited to visual symptoms. They may be very minimal, such as confusion or the smelling of a strange odor, or a pins-and-needles sensation in one arm, one leg, or both. The visual symptoms, however, may seem catastrophic, as in seeing bright stars, fortification spectra (see Figure 1 in Chapter 5), blind spots, or loss of vision in part of the visual field.

Associated Symptoms

The migraine attack may include a wide variety of symptoms occurring in association with the pain, such as discomfort from light, nausea, vomiting, and difficulty with urination. Cluster headache may be associated with tearing eyes, drooping eyelids, nasal congestion, and facial flushing. A person with glaucoma may experience clouding of the cornea and visual difficulties. In a patient with a brain hemorrhage, a stiff neck is one of the most prominent symptoms. Sudden loss of power in the arms or legs associated with a headache would suggest a stroke. Ringing in the ears or double-vision on one side may indicate a brain tumor. If a headache and a seizure occur simultaneously for the first time in a patient, it usually signifies a serious organic disease.

Sleep Patterns

Difficulty in falling asleep is indicative of anxiety. The physician should do a careful history to determine if stress or psychological factors may be producing the problem. Frequent or early waking is a pattern of depression. Migraine patients are rarely awakened by severe headache and are usually helped by sleep. Cluster headache patients, however, are frequently awakened by severe head pain and the intensity of the pain forces them into restless activity until the attack subsides.

Various Environmental Factors

Patients with migraine or muscle contraction headache frequently relate an increased frequency or an acute onset of the headache to emotionally or physically stressful events. After a lumbar puncture (spinal tap), pneumoencephalogram, or myelogram, there is often intensification of the headache when the head is raised. This is due to the absence of adequate cerebrospinal fluid, which places a pulling sensation on the intracranial structures. If the headache is due to a fever, tumor, or other organic cause, the pain may be intensified with sudden head movements, such as choking, coughing, sneezing, or straining with a bowel movement.

Sexual intercourse may trigger the sudden onset of a headache, particularly in those individuals susceptible to migraine or muscle contraction headache. Multiple factors, such as fatigue, loss of sleep, stress, menstruation, bright sunlight, and foods and drugs containing tyramine or other vasoactive substances, can increase the severity of migraine. High altitudes, alcohol, or missing a meal may also provoke a headache.

We recognize the importance of the patient's family relationships, occupation, social life, environmental stresses, sexual habits, and means of coping with stress. A detailed history of these factors is essential because they have special relevance to a person's headaches. One may uncover an underlying psychological illness that has been masked by the headache patient. Psychic and emotional symptoms combined will usually alert the physician to an underlying depression.

Occupational Triggers

Emotional factors, increased work loads, and stress on the job are frequent headache causes. There are certain occupations that predispose toward headache—those which involve dealing with the public under stress or working in a migraine-triggering environment. Abattoir workers, for instance, are subject to acute fever with intense headache as one of the symptoms. The nitrates to which munitions workers are exposed can cause vasodilation of the cerebral vessels and mimic vascular headache. Mechanics and others who work in poorly ventilated areas can get headaches from the carbon monoxide in the atmosphere. One young woman who worked at one of the pharmaceutical houses manufacturing birth control pills developed headaches because of inhaling estrogen.

Family History

Migraine is a familial disease while cluster headache is not. Depression also occurs in families. Depression often appears during "happy" periods such as Christmas. Brain tumors and simple tension headaches usually do not have any family relationship.

Relationship to Menstrual Cycle

Until the time of puberty, migraine occurs more frequently in males. With the onset of menses, it becomes more common in females. During pregnancy, most migraines will disappear by the third month, only to reappear after the child has been delivered. Many women suffer exclusively from menstrual migraine. Often, migraines will disappear with menopause. The administration of hormones in the post-menopausal period can prolong the headache syndrome. Conversely, migraine which occasionally appears for the first time with menopause may be improved by the injection of small amounts of estrogen.

Medical History

It is essential to obtain a very thorough medical history. It should be determined if the patient incurred a recent or remote head trauma. We have observed patients who suffered minimal blows to the head with resultant clots between the covering of the brain and the brain itself. Spinal tap, anesthesia, or other procedures can cause a limited headache. A history of seizures, one-sided headache, and neck stiffness should always alert the physician to the possibility of a weak blood vessel, aneurysm, or congenital malformation of a blood vessel.

Surgical History

A past history of tuberculosis may have significance, with a possible radiation to the brain. Any previous surgery or operations on the head would alert the physician to possible organic causes of the headache. Past surgery on a mole or tumor in any other part of the body should not be ignored.

Allergies

The possibility of a relationship between the headaches and seasonal allergies should be determined. The patient may experience increased headache associated with hayfever or seasonal allergic symptoms due to an increase in sensitivity of the blood vessels of the nose and sinuses. However, it has never been determined that migraine or other forms of headache result directly from allergic disease. Countless patients have had repeated sophisticated workups for allergies, including many tests with inherent risks. The currency and judiciousness of these tests, considered along with the history and current physical findings, should dictate to the physician whether or not these studies should be repeated. Headache may also be associated with hypothyroidism or anemia. There is no substitute for an adequate inventory of the headache patient, but it is not prudent to repeat expensive and potentially dangerous tests.

Past Medications

Past medications can be a key to the diagnosis as well as the treatment of the patient. For example, if ergotamine has helped the patient previously, we are probably dealing with migraine. If the patient has had a trial of antidepressants with some success, the likelihood of depression is increased. Therefore, a history of past medications and their success or failure yields a diagnostic and therapeutic clue to the management of the patient.

Present Medications

The current medications employed by the patient should also be inventoried. Many migraine or depressed patients take re-

serpine for their high blood pressure, which tends to promote
both headache and depression. Migraine may be increased in
frequency and severity by birth control pills. We know that
nitrates can activate migraine in certain susceptible people.
Indomethacin (Indocin) is another drug that can, on occasion,
cause chronic head pain. The physician should be thorough
in obtaining the drug history of the patient.

5

MIGRAINE HEADACHES

Case History 8

M.E., 32 years old, describes episodic headaches involving one side of her head. Her father and only son have a similar problem. As a child, she was easily carsick, found it difficult to play twirling games, and had recurrent episodes of unexplained vomiting without diarrhea, which puzzled the family pediatrician. Her headaches started at age 15 and have continued to the present. Menarche was at age 13.

The headaches appear monthly, starting three days pre-menses. She notes that initially there is a slight loss of vision in part of her visual field, following which she sees twinkling lights and a series of jagged lines, which she can sometimes draw on paper. These visual images appear in both eyes. Promptly thereafter, the images cease, and the headache begins. It is localized to one side of the head, but with different episodes may shift from side to side. The pain is severe and pounding, increasing with bending over or straining, and is not noticeably relieved by lying down. Shortly after the pain begins, she experiences significant nausea and may vomit repeatedly.

Bright lights and sound bother her. She must leave work and return home, where she retires to her bedroom, pulls the blind, and tries to sleep. If she can get to sleep, she may wake up free of headache. After about 24 hours the headache begins to wane and is usually gone by 48 hours; then she is left depleted, with a feeling of exhaustion. The patient notes that her headaches become more severe in the fall and spring, and may be precipitated by changes in barometric pressure.

M.E. is recognized by her co-workers as extremely competent and meticulous to a fault. She is compulsive about details and consistently checks the work of subordinates carefully. Her superiors recognize her as a woman of talent and have marked her for rapid advancement to an executive position.

Migraine is a vascular headache. The migraine headache is associated with changes in the size of the arteries inside and outside the brain. During the pre-headache phase, the blood vessels constrict. Common to all types of migraine is vascular dilation, representing the headache phase of migraine. Certain drugs can cause the blood vessels in a nonmigrainous person to react in a way similar to those of a migraine sufferer. Cerebral blood flow is thought to decrease during the pre-headache phase, or prodrome, and increase during the headache phase. Thermography has shown that there is increased blood flow to the painful area of the head during a migraine headache, but there can be a discrepancy between the time and space relationship of blood flow and migraine symptoms.

The blood vessels are thought to become inflamed as well as swollen. The pain in migraine headaches is believed to be caused by this inflammation, as well as by the pressure on the swollen walls of the blood vessels. They may swell and become inflamed due to changes in vasoactive substances. The factor unifying all of the migraine causes may be a problem in the metabolism of amines. A change in serotonin leads to the blood vessels' constriction. Less blood and, thus, less oxygen pass through the blood vessels. This is what happens during the prodrome of the migraine, with its accompanying neurological symptoms. The serotonin then changes again, and the blood vessels change from a constricted state to a dilated one, with the prodrome or aura ending, and pain starting. It is unknown why the different precipitating factors cause the change in the vasoactive chemicals around the brain. Immediately after a headache, the blood vessels go through a refractory period when they do not react to the headache triggers that would normally provoke an attack.

Migraine headaches vary greatly from person to person and may also vary from attack to attack in the individual. The headaches differ in intensity, frequency, and duration. Most often migraine headaches are unpredictable and do not establish a regular pattern. Migraine is derived from the Greek word "hemicrania" meaning "half of the head" because the headache is usually unilateral. In 70% of sufferers, it is experienced on one side of the head. The migraine headache can, however, be bilateral or shift across the forehead from side to side during an attack. An individual sufferer often finds the pain starting on the same side.

The pain of the migraine headache is generally described as recurrent and throbbing. It usually begins as a dull ache and gradually develops into a pulsating type of pain. The pain becomes throbbing as the blood pulses through the dilated arteries from the heart. The arteries in the painful area of the head become enlarged and can be seen throbbing. Then the blood vessels become thicker and more rigid and do not pulse. The pain becomes more constant and the location of the headache may be less specific. The headaches are separated by periods of freedom from pain.

The pain is often felt in the front or temporal areas, or it may settle behind the eye. It may radiate to other regions of the face or neck. In classical migraine, the pain often strikes the side of the head opposite the side of the aura. When the pain associated with migraine is felt in the neck and shoulder areas, it could partially be the result of the sufferer attempting to keep his head motionless, since a migraine headache's severity is increased with movement. Thus, a person can suffer from a combination of migraine and muscle contraction headache at the same time.

Most migraine sufferers get two to four headaches per month, but the frequency does vary greatly. Some people get a headache every few days, while others may get only one or two a year. Migraine headaches rarely strike every day. They generally last one or two days. Most migraine headaches last at least four hours, and very severe ones can last almost a week. The headaches can begin at any time of the day or night, and the sufferer often wakes up with one. Unlike other types of headache, migraine headaches rarely awaken a person from sleep.

The migraine headache may take different forms as one gets older. A young child may experience vomiting attacks without a headache. Many migraine sufferers are afflicted with motion sickness in their childhood. Around seven years of age, the headache is often added to the syndrome, and after puberty, the aura may appear. The headaches tend to decrease as one gets older. The vomiting aspect may subside once a person reaches middle age, and after menopause the headaches may disappear completely, or at least become less frequent and less severe. In some elderly people, the aura or other neurological symptoms may persist even after the headaches have stopped. The headaches can stop at any age for a period of months or years, for no apparent reason.

There are various types of migraine headaches, with *common* and *classical* being most prevalent. Both common migraine and classical migraine are thought to stem from biological abnormalities. The headache phase is similar in both types of migraine. However, classical migraine has a pre-headache phase known as an aura, or prodrome, which common migraine does not have. At times it is difficult to separate people into classical and common migraine groups, as some migraine sufferers exhibit symptoms of both. Approximately 35% of migraine sufferers have typical classical migraine with an aura that occurs 10 to 20 minutes before the headache.

The aura is not a precipitating factor of the migraine headache but an integral part of the headache itself. It is generally restricted to one side of the head or body, opposite the side of the headache. The visual and other neurological disturbances of the prodrome are thought to be the result of impaired blood circulation to the brain. The aura is most often visual, and the type of visual disturbance that occurs is dependent on which arteries are involved. Visual symptoms can involve a dimness or blind spot on one side that may spread until half of each field of vision is temporarily blinded. This partial blindness is called a scotoma. The visual image may be in the form of a fort with a zigzag shape, thus the name "fortification spectra" (see Figure 1). A visual aura can also involve flashing lights or a radiating bright spot on one side of the visual field. Tunnel vision, an impairment in peripheral vision, can also occur. An aura may include visual and/or auditory hallucinations. The "Alice in Wonderland" syndrome refers to the bizarre aura ascribed to Lewis Carroll, a migraine sufferer, which appears in his writings of Alice's adventures: "I'm very brave generally," he went on in a low voice, "only today I happen to have a headache" (*Through the Looking Glass*). Carroll must have experienced distortions in body shape as well as other disturbances of the senses. An aura may include strange odors, since disruptions of smell, taste, and touch can occur as well as disruptions in vision and hearing. An aura may also involve feelings of numbness or cold or a pins-and-needles sensation. Giddiness, muscular weakness, or disturbances of balance can take place. Occa-

Figure 1
Fortification Spectra Seen Before Migraine Attack

sionally, there is a speech difficulty. The problem usually lies
in finding or uttering the correct word, although, in rare instances, there is an inability to speak. The aura and accompanying neurological symptoms generally disappear when the
headache phase begins. Complicated migraine, however, refers to a type of migraine headache that involves permanent
neurological damage. A "migraine equivalent" is a condition
in which many of the cerebral symptoms falling under the
category of an aura occur without a headache following them.
This can occur in classical migraine in an elderly sufferer.

Ophthalmoplegic migraine and *hemiplegic migraine* are
rare conditions, which are considered to be more severe types
of classical migraine. In ophthalmoplegic migraine, the pain
usually surrounds the eyeball, and lasts from a few days to a
few months. There may be paralysis in the muscles surrounding
the eye. It is important to confirm the diagnosis of ophthalmoplegic migraine, as similar symptoms can be caused by
pressure on the nerves behind the eye. In hemiplegic migraine,
the sufferer may develop some temporary motor paralysis
and/or sensory disturbances on one side of the body, followed
in 10 to 90 minutes by the headache. This may be accompanied
by numbness or a pins-and-needles sensation. The neurological
symptoms usually leave when the headache appears. With
hemiplegic migraine, there is often a familial occurrence.

Abdominal migraine is a form of migraine in which the
pain is felt in the abdomen. It is a difficult syndrome to diagnose. The aura, nausea, and vomiting are all accompanying
factors. The pain can be very severe and last 12 to 18 hours.
The pain is similar to that of migraine in the head—throbbing
in nature in the beginning and becoming constant. Abdominal
migraine can switch to the more familiar migraine in the head
after a number of years. It usually responds better to anticonvulsant therapy than to medications normally used in migraine
treatment.

Facial migraine is a variant of migraine that affects the

face below the eye rather than the head. The pain spreads to the ear, nose, cheek, or jaw. It is also referred to as a "lower half" headache.

Basilar artery migraine is a very rare form of migraine in which the headache is accompanied by dizziness, confusion, or a lack of balance. Sudden onset and transient visual disturbances on both sides, the inability to speak properly, a ringing in the ears, and vomiting are other associated symptoms. The throbbing headache occurs in the back of the head. It strikes mainly young adult women and adolescent girls. Basilar artery migraine has a strong relationship to hormonal influences. With aging, basilar artery migraine may be replaced by more common forms of vascular headache.

Another rare type of migraine is *retinal migraine*, which first involves a temporary, partial, or complete loss of vision in one eye. It is followed by a dull ache behind that eye, which may then spread to the rest of the head.

The migraine headache is accompanied by a wide range of symptoms affecting many parts of the body, including the eyes and gastrointestinal tract (see Figure 2). Some of the associated symptoms may occur considerably before the headache, while others occur throughout the attack. Between migraine headaches, the sufferer generally has no abnormal physical symptoms. Nausea and vomiting accompany 90% of migraine headaches. This is the reason migraines are so often referred to as "sick" headaches. Loss of appetite and diarrhea may also be present, with resultant extreme weakness. The various biochemical changes that occur with a migraine headache can result in mood changes. Before a migraine attack there is often a feeling of euphoria and the sufferer may have a great surge of energy. Some people, however, feel irritable and tense before an attack. The headache is often followed by exhaustion and feelings of depression. Depression and migraine are often seen together. It is estimated that nearly half of all headaches are accompanied by chronic depression, which

Migraine

A. The aura

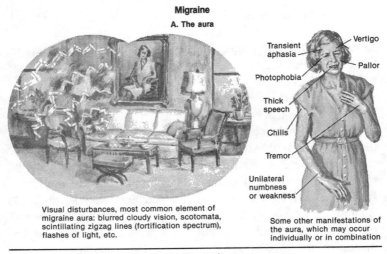

Visual disturbances, most common element of migraine aura: blurred cloudy vision, scotomata, scintillating zigzag lines (fortification spectrum), flashes of light, etc.

Transient aphasia
Photophobia
Thick speech
Chills
Tremor
Unilateral numbness or weakness

Vertigo
Pallor

Some other manifestations of the aura, which may occur individually or in combination

B. The attack

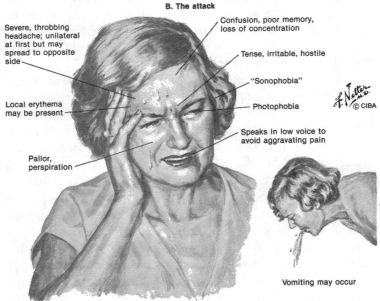

Severe, throbbing headache; unilateral at first but may spread to opposite side

Local erythema may be present

Pallor, perspiration

Confusion, poor memory, loss of concentration

Tense, irritable, hostile

"Sonophobia"

Photophobia

Speaks in low voice to avoid aggravating pain

Vomiting may occur

Figure 2

Reprinted by permission from *Clinical Symposia: CIBA*, Vol. 33, No. 2, 1981.

usually involves a sleep disturbance as well. A migraine headache may be associated with an inability to concentrate. A person suffering from a migraine headache usually prefers to lie down in a quiet, dark room. During an attack, the migraineur becomes very sensitive to light (photophobia) and noise (phonophobia). The lack of tolerance for loud noises that often accompanies the headache may be associated with distorted hearing, in which voices sound unnatural. Some of the possible accompanying vasomotor signs include a change in pulse rate, face pallor, and a feeling of faintness. Cold hands and feet are common during a migraine attack. Other symptoms include sweating, nasal congestion and swelling, and redness or tearing of the eyes. Tenderness of the scalp in the area of the headache is also common. Fluid retention is often associated with the headache phase. There can be local or generalized swelling. As the headache subsides, the excess body fluid is usually excreted.

Migraine Profile

A minimum of eight to 12 million Americans suffer from migraine headaches. Approximately 70% of migraine sufferers report a family history of the disorder. It is not known exactly how the familial nature of migraine operates, although it is believed that the predisposition or susceptibility to migraine is inherited. One school of thought theorizes that it passes from generation to generation through a gene. There might also be a cultural inheritance, with a child imitating his parent's headache pattern. Migraine headaches may begin in childhood; most often they begin when the patient is in his twenties or thirties. They rarely strike a person over 50 years of age. Sixty percent of all migraine sufferers are women. This may be due to hormonal influences in women. However, a reluctance on the part of men to report their migraine pain and seek medical aid may also be a factor making for a greater prevalence of *known* cases in women.

There is not really one specific migraine personality. Psychological research into the personalities of migraine sufferers has shown that they cannot be grouped together into any specific category. Many of the following personality characteristics and traits can be used only as clues in diagnosing migraine headaches. Not all migraine sufferers will have them, just as, conversely, not all people with these personality traits suffer from migraine headaches. Migraine sufferers have been described as compulsive, rigid perfectionists. They are often extremely neat, orderly, and well-groomed. The migraineur is thought to be high-strung, very analytical, conscientious, meticulous, and a quick talker. He usually knows the precise frequency, location, and duration of his headaches and may well provide the consulting physician with carefully prepared lists of this information. Many sufferers find it difficult to relax and are very reactive to stressful situations. Furthermore, they tend to build environments with too many demands and are very sensitive to this overload. Migraine sufferers are often thought to repress emotions such as anger, hostility, or feelings of inadequacy. They prefer to be in control of the situation and do not like uncertainty. They tend to set very high standards for themselves and others. Migraine sufferers have long been considered some of the brightest, most ambitious, and most active achievers of the world. This is a logical conclusion when one examines the following list of famous people who have suffered from migraine headaches: Julius Caesar, Joan of Arc, Peter the Great, Cervantes, Pascal, Nietzsche, Charles Darwin, Chopin, Leo Tolstoy, Edgar Allan Poe, Tchaikovsky, Queen Mary Tudor, Virginia Woolf, Thomas Jefferson, Robert E. Lee, Ulysses S. Grant, Sigmund Freud, Alfred Nobel, Karl Marx, Lewis Carroll, and George Bernard Shaw. It is argued that migraine sufferers are not necessarily more intelligent, as popularly believed, but possibly the more intelligent sufferers are more likely to seek medical help.

Precipitating Factors

A migraineur is thought to have a predisposition toward migraine headaches, but this predisposition must be activated or "triggered" by a number of outside factors. The migraine sufferer's blood vessels are thought to be more reactive to various triggers than those of a nonmigrainous person. Both biological and emotional factors can trigger a migraine headache. Many of the precipitating factors involve stress, hormones, diet, sleep patterns, and environmental and physical factors. The triggers set off the headache process in susceptible individuals. Often, a single factor will not provoke a migraine, while a combination of triggers will set off an attack. In order to prevent the attacks, the migraine sufferer must be able to identify his precipitating factors. A migraine sufferer can prevent at least some of his headaches by recognizing and avoiding his individual triggers. Migraine headaches may decrease in frequency and severity with increasing age as the blood vessels become less reactive to precipitating factors. Many people, however, have migraines that do not relate to any external factors.

Stress

Events causing emotional stress can trigger a migraine headache. It is one of the most common precipitating factors of migraine. Migraine sufferers are thought to be highly responsive emotionally, reacting quickly and easily to stress. In times of emotional stress, certain chemicals are released that provoke the vascular changes that cause a migraine headache. The attacks become more frequent in periods of increased stress. Factors related to stress include anxiety, worry, shock, depression, excitement, and mental fatigue. Repressed emotions can also precipitate migraine headaches, and the muscle tension often brought on by stress situations can add to the severity of the headache. After a stressful period there may be a letdown which can, in itself, trigger a migraine headache. The arteries may be constricted by prolonged stress, and when the individual is finally able to relax, the blood vessels may dilate, causing the headache. This may be one reason for weekend headaches. Attacks occurring during a relaxation period, after stress, can often be helped by modifying the stressful periods and keeping busier during leisure times.

Hormones

Case History 9

D.G., aged 27, started having headaches at age 14. The pain is unilateral, affecting either the right or left temple and the area above the eyes. The headaches have increased in frequency in the past two years. Previously, they occurred two to three times per year; now they occur two to three times per week. Originally, the headaches lasted six to eight hours, but now they continue for two to three days. The pain is described as a moderate to severe pounding. The headaches are incapacitating and are associated with nausea, vomiting, photophobia, and occasional blurred vision. The patient's sleep pattern has not been affected. She states that she is a perfectionist and compulsive. Her mother and aunt both have a history of migraine. The medical and surgical histories are negative. The patient states that the ingestion of alcohol increases the severity of the headaches. The headaches are more severe with menses. The patient started birth control pills (Ovral) two years ago.

The majority of migraine sufferers are women in the period between their first menses and menopause. This suggests a strong hormonal influence in migraine headaches. The precipitating factors related to hormones include menstruation and the pre-menstrual period, hormonal treatment during menopause, and the use of oral contraceptives.

Although there is some controversy over this subject, a number of observations point to the likelihood that some of the hormone changes accompanying menstruation are linked to migraine headaches in some women. Changes in the woman's body occur constantly in relation to the hormonal cycle. The levels of the female hormones, estrogen and progesterone, fall before the onset of menstruation. Fluid retention often accompanies the migraine precipitated by hormonal factors. Approximately 70% of women migraine sufferers find some of their headaches occurring just before, during, or soon after their menstrual periods. It is argued that since this sensitive time includes the pre-menstrual week, the menstrual week, and the week following the period, or three out of four weeks in the month, many of the headaches would have occurred anyway, regardless of hormonal influences. However, the increased onset of migraine headaches in women after puberty and the decrease of migraine headache after menopause and during pregnancy are evidence supporting the influence of hormones in migraine headaches.

Until puberty, the number of boys and girls who suffer from migraine is about equal. After puberty, the incidence of migraine increases dramatically in girls, and females continue to outnumber males until after menopause, when the numbers become equal again. Migraine disappears after menopause in about 75% of women. The lessening of migraine after menopause is due primarily to the decrease in female hormones in the body, but the prescription of female hormones during menopause may prevent this natural decline. The attacks are then prolonged and may even increase in frequency and severity. Migraine headaches tend to become less frequent and less severe during pregnancy. The majority of women migraine sufferers' headaches subside by the third month of pregnancy. Conversely, a few women first develop migraine during a pregnancy.

Throughout a woman's monthly cycle, the levels of various hormones are continually changing to permit ovulation to occur, followed by menstruation or pregnancy. These hormones include progesterone, estrogen, and pituitary hormones. All women have individual variations in these levels from day to day. Migraine headaches seem to occur primarily when progesterone is not secreted. The estrogen levels are generally high in the middle of the menstrual cycle and during or just after the menstrual period. Progesterone is secreted during the second half of the menstrual cycle. Progesterone is also secreted throughout pregnancy. It is not known why hormonal changes in the body may cause changes in the substances around the brain leading to vasodilation of the blood vessels. Hormonal treatment with progesterone has been tried with variable results. It was theorized that raising the progesterone level with medications, as occurs naturally during pregnancy, could bring relief from migraine headaches.

Oral contraceptives and post-menopausal hormones generally increase the frequency, severity, and duration of migraine headaches. They contain the two female hormones, progesterone and estrogen, in varying proportions. Oral contraceptives increase the concentration of female hormones in the body. They can induce headaches even in previously migraine-free women. As many as 40% of women on oral contraceptives suffer from headaches. Many of the women taking oral contraceptives who experience headaches for the first time suffer from a typical migraine type of headache—unilateral, throbbing, and accompanied by nausea and vomiting. Others experience less typical migraines, with the pain felt as pressure throughout the head, and in some women the headache is accompanied by depression, irritability, or sleeplessness. Withdrawal of the oral contraceptives and other female hormones often leads to a dramatic improvement in migraine headaches. Conversely, in a few women, headaches improve while using these hormones. It is generally considered better for migraine sufferers not to use oral contraceptives or other female hormones. The use of oral contraceptives in migraine sufferers can lead to complications such as strokes or other serious illnesses.

Diet

Plinius, a Greek philosopher, taught that fresh dates intoxicate and induce headaches, probably because they contain the vasoactive substance tyramine. Dietary factors are a major precipitating cause in migraine headache problems. Approximately 30% of migraine sufferers' headaches are provoked by dietary factors. There are, however, other factors that will also trigger migraine headaches in these people. The precipitating factors related to diet include consumption of certain foods or alcohol, prolonged lack of food, or irregular meals. Diet is one trigger mechanism of migraine headaches that can be controlled or modified.

So many factors can trigger a migraine attack that it is difficult to pinpoint only one or two or three. However, most migraineurs will name stress, hormonal changes, and diet as the most troublesome. Diet can trigger an attack through any one of a large group of amines, nitrates, nitrites, and other substances found in food, so that the sufferer might be well advised to avoid eating. But fasting, too, can provoke a migraine attack. Indeed, some volunteers for headache research fast in order to bring on the headache needed for the studies.

There appears to be a link between blood sugar level and migraine. Changes in the blood sugar level may influence the nerves that control the size of blood vessels. When the blood sugar level is high, as in pregnancy, diabetes, or rapid weight gain, migraine attacks are less frequent. In contrast, migraine attacks tend to increase when the blood sugar level is low. Prolonged lack of food due to fasting or dieting, or even irregular or delayed meals, can trigger migraine headaches in many people. Migraineurs whose headaches are precipitated by skipping a meal should be sure to eat at regular intervals. Migraine headaches often occur in the early morning and may be partially caused by a low blood sugar level. A protein snack before bed can help to relieve this situation. Changes in the eating routine can also provoke a migraine headache. This often occurs on weekends when a person who normally eats breakfast may sleep late and skip or delay the morning meal. To avoid this, the susceptible migraine sufferer should be sure to have some sort of breakfast at a regular time each day. This may involve waking up early on the weekend, having breakfast, and then going back to sleep. When a nonmigrainous person begins to get a headache after missing or delaying a meal, eating will usually relieve the headache symptom. However, when this situation arises with the migraine sufferer, eating will not abort the beginning headache. Careful timing of meals can prevent this situation. Lack of food can also intensify an already-existing headache, so it is a good idea to eat at least small amounts of food during an attack, if possible.

The body of a migraine sufferer has difficulty adapting to certain foods, and most of these foods contain tyramine. Migraineurs have a chemical sensitivity to foods containing tyramine because it is a vasoactive amine. Tyramine provokes certain hormonal and circulatory changes in the migrainous person's body. Past studies have indicated that these people metabolize tyramine differently from nonmigrainous people. Chocolate, however, is the most common dietary migraine trigger, although it contains little or no tyramine. Another amine, beta-phenylethylamine, is found in chocolate and has been identified as a trigger of migraine headaches. It falls into the same group of amines as tyramine. Both have a direct action on the blood vessels. Some people cannot tolerate tyramine or beta-phenylethylamine in their diets. Histamine is another powerful vasodilator that can be a source of dietary migraine. One theory proposes that the migraine sufferer lacks certain enzymes that will rid the body of these amines; thus, they remain in the blood or tissues and affect the blood vessels and trigger migraine headaches.

Certain foods and beverages contain more than one of the vasoactive substances. Migraine headaches triggered by many alcoholic beverages and cheeses may be caused by the combined effect of more than one of the vasoactive chemicals. There can also be varying amounts of these amines in different brands or types of a food product. For instance, different cheeses contain different quantities of tyramine. The more aged types, such as Brie, Camembert, Cheddar, Stilton, Emmentaler, Gruyere, and Blue Cheese, contain more tyramine and thus can more easily trigger a migraine headache. The most common precipitating foods include, in order of prevalence, chocolate, cheeses and other dairy products, citrus fruits, and alcohol. These foods and beverages trigger headaches only in certain migraine sufferers and generally not in the nonmigrainous person.

As indicated above, alcohol can provoke migraine headaches. This is especially true if the sufferer is in a migraine phase. Already-existing migraine headaches are intensified by alcohol, which is a vasodilator and thus a trigger of migraine headaches. Alcoholic beverages such as red wines contain large amounts of tyramine. Histamine is another vasodilating amine found in some wines and champagne. Some migraine sufferers are able to drink white wines without precipitating a headache, while an attack may follow a glass of red wine. Beer, red wine, bourbon, gin, or any fermented beverage may trigger migraine headaches. Alcoholic beverages that do not generally provoke headaches include white and rosé wines, brandy, cordials, rum, and scotch. A hangover headache is also caused by vasodilation of the blood vessels, but usually after the consumption of a much greater quantity of alcohol than with the migraine headache triggered by alcohol. Other factors besides tyramine or vasodilation may be related to the hangover headache, such as fatigue, social stress, dehydration, and a smoke-filled atmosphere. The blood sugar level falls after the consumption of large amounts of alcohol, which may also contribute to the headache.

Elimination of foods with vasoactive qualities from the diet can reduce many headache problems. The following dietary restrictions are recommended for the migraineur (see also Appendix):

AVOID:

Ripened cheeses, such as Cheddar, Emmentaler, Gruyere, Stilton, Brie, and Camembert (Permissible cheeses: American, cottage cheese, cream cheese, and Velveeta)

Herring

Chocolate

Vinegar (White vinegar is permissible)

Any pickled, fermented, or marinated foods

Sour cream or yogurt

Nuts, peanut butter, seeds (Sunflower, sesame, pumpkin, etc.)

Hot fresh breads, raised coffeecakes, and doughnuts

Pods of broad beans (Lima, navy, and pea pods)

Any foods containing large amounts of monosodium glutamate (e.g., Chinese foods)

Onions

Canned figs

Citrus fruits (Not more than one orange per day)

Bananas (Not more than one-half banana per day)

Pizza

Pork (Not more than two or three times per week)

Excessive quantities of tea, coffee, or cola beverages (Not more than four cups per day)

Avocado

Fermented sausage (Bologna, salami, Pepperoni, summer sausage, and hot dogs)

Chicken liver

All alcoholic beverages (If you must drink, not more than two drinks. The following are suggested drinks: Haute sauterne, Riesling, Seagram's VO, Cutty Sark, and vodka)

Avoiding foods and beverages known to trigger migraine headaches may reduce the frequency and intensity of the head pain. Keeping a careful dietary record can accurately pinpoint the foods that may trigger the migraine headache in the individual sufferer. A dietary record should include food intake and activities for the day preceding each attack. If an individual observes that certain foods and drinks precipitate migraine headaches, he should certainly avoid them.

Sleep Pattern

The precipitating factors of headache related to sleep pattern include late rising, physical fatigue, and the use of sleeping pills. Sleeping too long, too little, or too deeply can provoke a migraine headache. Oversleeping can precipitate headaches in certain migraine sufferers. The depth of respiration decreases during some phases of sleep. Carbon dioxide, which can dilate blood vessels, may accumulate in the blood. Migraine headaches are associated with rapid eye movement (REM) sleep. Too much sleep can lead to a change in the body's blood sugar level as well, provoking a migraine headache. Those migraineurs who experience "weekend" headaches or headaches precipitated by oversleeping should try to awaken at the same time on weekends as they do during the week and to maintain a regular sleep pattern throughout the entire week. Moreover, it is essential for the migraine sufferer to get enough sleep, as fatigue can provoke a headache. In fact, fatigue is one of the most common triggers of migraine headaches.

Environmental and Physical Factors

The environmental factors that can provoke a migraine headache are extremely variable and affect only a small proportion of migraine sufferers. Environmental factors that can trigger a migraine include a change in climate or weather (such as a change in humidity or temperature), a change in altitude or barometric pressure, high winds, traveling, or a change in routine. Other environmental triggers include a bright or flickering light (sunlight reflections, glare, fluorescent lighting, television, or movies), extremes of heat and sound, and intense smells or vapors.

Weather changes can cause biological changes in the body's chemical balance and thus precipitate a migraine headache in some sensitive people. Weather conditions can also increase the severity of a headache induced by other factors. Extreme cold as well as very humid weather conditions have been known to trigger migraine headaches. A very dry and dusty atmosphere can also precipitate a migraine. When too many electrically charged dust particles are inhaled, it is thought that certain vasoactive chemicals are released, thus triggering a headache. These particles may also provoke the migraine headaches associated with certain winds and storms or with crowding in a stuffy room. A change in barometric pressure can trigger a migraine headache. The reduction of oxygen causes the blood and blood vessels to compensate. The scalp arteries swell, as they are extremely sensitive to the pressure of oxygen in the blood, especially to sudden changes, such as those that occur with flying in an airplane or sea diving. People living or traveling at high elevations can experience similar headaches.

Any changes in a migraineur's environment that involve adjustment and adaptation can provoke a headache. Changing schools or jobs requires a great deal of adaptation, resulting in difficulty for the migraine sufferer. Travel may provoke migraine headaches because of the change in routine or diet as well as the new environmental and atmospheric conditions. Many migraineurs are sensitive to travel- and seasickness. The jarring motion of a car, train, or boat can trigger a headache.

Many migraine sufferers are very sensitive to light, especially to glare. Bright lights are more likely to trigger migraine headaches when they are of a "flickering" quality, and a slow flicker is usually more irritating than a more rapid one. It is believed that some people have more excitable brain cells in response to light than others. A dazzling, flickering type of light can be found in light reflected on snow, sand, or water, or through clouds. Some fluorescent lighting or the light that flickers from television and movie screens may have a similar effect. The use of polaroid lenses in these glaring conditions can be helpful.

Certain fumes and vapors can cause the blood vessels of the susceptible person to swell and dilate, triggering a migraine headache. Carbon monoxide poisoning from a poorly ventilated environment can provoke a headache. Faulty furnaces in winter can be responsible for such fumes. The nitrites used in explosives can trigger a headache in susceptible persons who are employed in munitions plants. Smoking can provoke or intensify a headache. It can cause biological changes in the blood and blood vessels. Just being in a smoke-filled environment can provoke a headache in susceptible people. Loud and irritating noises can also precipitate migraine headaches. This may be associated with stress as well as change in environmental conditions.

Many physical factors can also trigger migraine headaches, including overexertion such as bending, straining, or lifting; high blood pressure; toothache; or localized head or neck pains. These factors have been discussed in greater detail in previous sections.

Treatment of Migraine

Migraine headaches are probably the most difficult type of headache to treat. The exact cause of migraine is not known; thus, there is no distinct "cure." It is unlikely that one all-purpose treatment will be discovered that will "cure" all migraine patients. It is usually possible to bring the headaches under control and reduce their intensity and frequency. It is difficult to terminate them completely. There is probably more than one cause for the attacks. The triggers for each patient, as well as the characteristics of his headaches, are individual and vary greatly among people. Therefore, solving each headache problem involves choosing from the various types of treatment available and accounting for the individuality of the migraine headache condition. A variety of treatments may be necessary. Treatment of a migraine headache problem generally involves both attacking the pain of the migraine headache itself and identifying the underlying cause of the migraine pain and attempting to eliminate it. The physician initially tries to reduce the frequency and severity of the headaches, usually with medication. The second phase, finding the cause of the headache, is more difficult because it may be due to many factors.

General Measures

It is necessary to identify as many of the individual's migraine triggers as possible. You can be of help to yourself and the doctor by keeping a headache calendar to identify the precipitating factors (see below). The record should include the date and time of each headache; characteristics of the headache itself; food, drug, and beverage intake for the day before the headache, and the relationship of the headache to one's menstrual cycle or any other physical or environmental factors. A sample calendar and directions follow:

Headache Calendar

Patient's Name:
Date Started:

DATE	TIME END (Insert hr. and A.M./P.M.) ONSET	(*1) SEVERITY OF HEADACHE	(*2) RELIEF OF HEADACHE	MEDICATION TAKEN AND DOSAGE	(*3) PSYCHIC AND PHYSICAL FACTORS	(*4) FOOD AND DRINK EXCESSES

Directions for Using the Headache Calendar:

Date: Record the date each time you have a headache.

Time/Onset: Put down the hour (7:00 A.M., for example) when your headache started.

Time/End: Record the hour when your headache ended.

Severity of Headache: Record if the headache is mild, moderate, severe. The following scale is a guide:

SEVERITY SCALE

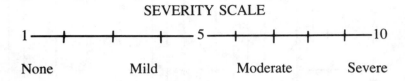

None   **Mild**   **Moderate**   **Severe**

Medication Taken and Dosage: Record what medication you took and how much you took each time. Indicate under "total" how many doses you took during the headache.

Relief of Headache: Record how effective the medication was, using these terms: no relief, mild, moderate, complete (see scale).

RELIEF SCALE

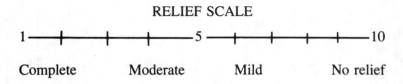

Complete   **Moderate**   **Mild**   **No relief**

Psychic and Physical Factors: Record anything you feel may have helped to trigger your headache. For example:

Emotional upset (family, friends, occupation)
Business problem (reversal, success)
Vacation days or weekends
Oversleeping
Strenuous exercise or labor
High altitude
Anticipation anxiety
Crisis (or post-crisis period)
Menstrual days
Physical illness
Illness in family
Change in weather
Fasting or missing a meal
New job or move

Food and Drink Excesses: Record foods you recently ate which may have helped to trigger your headache. For example:

Cheese or pizza
Chocolate
Vinegar
Fermented foods (e.g., sour cream, yogurt, pickled or marinated foods)
Herring
Fresh baked yeast products
Nuts (e.g., peanut butter)
Monosodium glutamate (e.g., Chinese foods)
Broad bean pods
Onions
Canned figs
Citrus fruits
Avocado
Bananas
Chicken liver
Pork
Cured cold cuts (sausage)
Coffee, tea, cola beverages
Wine
Beer
Alcohol

Once the provoking factors have been identified, avoiding the foods, beverages, medications, activities, and circumstances known to trigger the individual's headaches can prevent or lessen the attacks. Discontinuing oral contraceptives or other hormones, for instance, can have a dramatic effect in controlling the headache problem.

Helping the patient to adjust his lifestyle may offer some relief of the headache problem. With good planning, the migraine sufferer can learn to pace his life more evenly, thus minimizing the extremes of stress and leisure times. Adjusting the living pattern toward a steady pace, reducing stress, and learning to relax can reduce the number of migraine headaches. Attention must be paid to the role of fatigue and chronic stress in order to help a large number of migraine sufferers. For this reason, hypnosis, yoga, biofeedback, transcendental meditation, or other forms of relaxation training have benefited many migraine sufferers.

Another general measure involves keeping a regular routine. This includes waking at the same time every day and never oversleeping. It is also necessary to eat meals at regular intervals throughout the day. Some general measures for helping the migraine headache once it has begun include relaxing in a quiet, dark room with the head slightly elevated, and applying cold compresses to the head and heat to the neck. Resting without distraction in a quiet, dark place can greatly reduce the intensity and duration of the migraine headache. Local pressure or pressure on the temporal artery can offer some pain relief, and massaging the scalp and neck muscles is often found to be soothing.

Relief of the Attack

There is a large group of medications from which the physician may choose in an attempt to control migraine headache problems. There are more than eight medications used in the treatment of migraine headaches, as well as combinations and various dosages of each. With all of these possibilities, it often requires a number of trials to determine the best combination of medications for the individual sufferer. In deciding on the appropriate therapy for each person, the physician must weigh the benefits against the possible side effects. It must be remembered that individuals vary greatly in their responses to medications. The effectiveness of a particular form of treatment is partially dependent on the patient's judgment and cooperation. There is no specific pain reliever that is effective and safe for all people, nor is there one drug that will block

all aspects of inflammation. A combination of medications
may be necessary.

As no single cause of migraine headaches has been isolated, there is not one approach to "cure." It must be recognized that various factors contribute to the migraine headache,
such as hereditary susceptibility and the precipitating factors
for each individual headache. Thus, the various medications
approach the problem from different directions. Some medications raise the pain threshold, or the point at which a person
feels pain; some reduce the tension that increases the sensation
of pain; and some act on the physiological mechanism that
produces the pain. There are medications that kill the pain,
those that prevent the blood vessels from swelling, and those
that prevent a change in the substances in the brain that would
normally undergo a change during a migraine headache. Medications are used to decrease the action of vasoactive substances, stabilize the membranes, and reduce vasomotor
activity and inflammation. Most migraine sufferers require
some form of treatment that affects the blood vessels, i.e.,
vasoactive medications. Antiserotonin and antihistamine substances interfere with the action of the vasoactive amines.
Aspirin also indirectly affects the release of vasoactive substances.

The goal of migraine treatment is twofold—to relieve the
pain of acute attacks and to prevent future attacks. In line with
this, the two approaches to solving the headache problem are
abortive therapy and prophylactic, or preventive, therapy. The
abortive approach involves attempting to stop the migraine as
it is starting, while the prophylactic method aims at preventing
the headache from ever having a chance to start. At times,
abortive and prophylactic therapies are used together. A patient
may be on prophylactic medication which prevents most headaches, but when one does break through, the patient takes an
abortive drug to relieve the acute attack.

Abortive Approach

The abortive, or symptomatic, mode of therapy works well for the infrequent migraine headache. Abortive medications are used to treat the symptoms, pain, and associated discomforts of the acute attack. Abortive therapy involves interrupting the headache as it is about to begin. Medication must be taken at the first signal of a headache. Abortive therapy is most effective if the migraines occur predictably or infrequently. There can be a problem with abortive-type therapy if the headaches are too frequent, as most abortive medications have side effects and can themselves cause headaches.

Ergotamine tartrate is commonly prescribed as an abortive medication. Most medications used for the acute migraine headache contain ergotamine tartrate and are not painkillers. Ergotamine tartrate treats the symptoms of migraine but does not generally prevent the headache from occurring. It is a powerful drug isolated from ergot, which is derived from a fungus and is a derivative of lysergic acid (LSD). Ergotamine tartrate is chemically related to serotonin and has a similar effect on the blood vessels. Medications with ergotamine tartrate are vasoconstrictors and work specifically on the dilation of the extracranial arteries. However, they do not help headaches caused by factors other than vascular changes. Ergotamine tartrate may also reduce the arterial pulsation. It constricts the large arteries of the scalp, but in order to be effective, it must be used before the arteries have become too dilated.

Ergotamine tartrate must be taken before the head pain reaches its peak, as there is no treatment that is effective once the headache is fully developed. Therefore, the migraine sufferer who utilizes this type of medication should carry it with him at all times. The earlier the drug is taken in the attack, the greater the chances of aborting the headache. A rather large dose of ergotamine tartrate should be taken as soon as the sufferer suspects the onset of a migraine headache, thus accomplishing a rapid constriction of the arteries. The aura in classical migraine is a warning sign of the impending headache and indicates that medication should be taken immediately. Although sufferers of common migraine do not experience an aura before the head pain, they may also find ergotamine tartrate effective in aborting their headaches. Again, it must be taken at the first sign of any head pain. Those patients with common migraine who experience mood changes or any other symptoms before a migraine attack should utilize them as a warning to try to abort the attack.

A migraine headache can be prolonged if treatment is not taken early enough or if too much ergotamine tartrate is taken. If the first dose of ergotamine tartrate does not take effect, a second dose may be taken 30 to 45 minutes later. If it is going to abort the headache, it generally will do so within the hour. Thus, repeated doses will not bring further relief but may instead be dangerous and may even intensify the headache through excessive amounts of ergotamine tartrate. There should be a four-day waiting period between doses. Ergotamine abuse is very common. This can lead to ergot toxicity and a cycle of constant headaches. Symptoms of toxicity are common when more than 10 milligrams of ergotamine tartrate are taken per week. Other complications resulting from too much ergotamine tartrate are seizures and hallucinations. It should not be taken by people whose circulation is impaired in the arms and legs, or by those who suffer from peripheral vascular disease.

Ergotamine tartrate can be prescribed in various ways: orally, rectally, under the tongue, injected in the muscle or vein, or by inhalation. Each form has its advantages and disadvantages, and migraine sufferers have their own individual preferences. Injection is the quickest way for the medication to work in the individual's system. Suppositories are helpful when the patient is also suffering from nausea and vomiting and is unable to keep a pill down. Pills are the most convenient method for many people, as they can be taken at any time or any place. However, drugs given by mouth are thought to be less effective than those given by injection, suppository, or inhalation. Drug absorption may be impaired. Many believe that the stomach becomes inactive early in a migraine attack.

Ergotamine tartrate is often combined with other drugs to make it easier for the patient to sleep, to relieve anxiety, or to raise the pain threshold. These include analgesics, sedatives, and barbiturates. It may also be combined with drugs that reduce the nausea and vomiting associated with migraine headaches. Combining ergot with certain belladonna alkaloids, which are smooth-muscle relaxants, will help relieve the intestinal upheaval. It is often combined with caffeine since both ergotamine tartrate and caffeine constrict the blood vessels. Caffeine may also facilitate the absorption of ergotamine tartrate. Cafergot is a medication that combines caffeine and ergotamine tartrate. The two are also combined with the compound cyclizine to form Migral, which relieves the vomiting as well as the head pain. Wigraine is a combination medication containing ergotamine, caffeine, phenacetin, and belladonna. Cafergot, Migral, and Wigraine are all oral medications, as is Gynergen (a drug containing ergotamine alone). Gynergen can also be given as an intramuscular injection, as can Dihydroergotamine (DHE-45). Ergomar and Ergostat are medications containing ergotamine tartrate alone, and are taken sublingually, that is, under the tongue. Medihaler-Ergotamine is another migraine drug containing ergotamine. It is administered by inhalation. Cafergot, Cafergot-PB, and Wigraine may also be taken rectally by suppository.

Ergotamine tartrate is the most consistently effective treatment for acute migraine headaches. It also has the most prolonged effect. However, it must be taken with care, in moderation, and only by those migraine sufferers who can tolerate this powerful drug. It should not be taken by children and is contraindicated in patients with circulatory or cardiac problems and those who are pregnant. Some of the side effects of ergotamine tartrate are nausea, vomiting, diarrhea, numbness or tingling in the arms or legs, coldness or pallor in the hands and feet, leg cramps or weakness, and chest pain. A compound containing isometheptene mucate, dichloralphenazone, and acetaminophen (Midrin) is effective in aborting migraine. It is especially useful in patients who cannot tolerate ergotamine or who have peripheral vascular or cardiac disease, which limits the use of ergotamine. There are still contraindications to the use of Midrin in patients who have cardiac and peripheral vascular disease, but the use of this drug carries a much lesser risk than ergotamine. We consistently use isometheptene in patients who have a tendency to take ergotamine on a daily basis and thereby get rebound headaches. There is no rebound phenomenon from this drug.

Analgesics raise the pain threshold, lessening the pain sensation, but are not thought to affect the cause of the headache. The two most commonly used simple analgesics are aspirin and acetaminophen. Aspirin works as an analgesic and antipyretic, and may also have an anti-inflammatory effect. Analgesics may be used for the mild and infrequent migraine headache. They generally have little effect on the deep, throbbing pain of most migraine headaches. However, they do dull the pain of the occasional "normal" headache. Analgesics cannot be taken safely every day. Steroids are sometimes used to end a prolonged migraine headache.

Prophylactic Approach

The prophylactic approach to migraine headache control attempts to alter the biological or emotional factors that cause the attack, even before the pain or associated symptoms begin. Through prophylactic therapy, the physician attempts to prevent the headache from starting. With the prophylactic mode of therapy, the patient must take medication every day or every few hours. Thus, a patient must have headaches frequently enough to warrant this type of treatment—at least three to four migraine headaches per month. Many prophylactic medications, however, can be taken every day without the increased risk associated with abortive medications taken daily. Indeed, medications found to be effective in reducing the frequency of migraine headaches may be taken prophylactically two or three times a day. If a total cessation of the headaches is accomplished with prophylactic therapy, a gradual withdrawal of medication is often attempted. The primary groups of medications used in long-term treatment of migraine headaches are tranquilizers, antidepressants, and drugs that specifically act on the changes occurring with a migraine headache.

Propranolol (Inderal), a medication primarily used in the past for treating heart problems, is the most effective prophylactic therapy for migraine. It has recently been approved by the Food and Drug Administration as an effective treatment for migraine headaches. In fact, it is now the drug of choice in preventive therapy. Propranolol is a vasoactive medication that prevents cranial vasodilation. It blocks beta-receptors, thus decreasing the effect of stress or excitement, and it reduces the amount of blood pumped, lowering the blood pressure, which would normally increase with such stimulation. Dosages must be as high as 80 to 240 mg per day to be effective. Its use is not associated with the rebound headaches often accompanying such drugs as methysergide, nor is there a need for increasing dosages as with other preparations. Potential side effects include fatigue, gastrointestinal or heart problems, asthma attacks, or metabolic actions; thus, patients taking this drug must be closely monitored. Propranolol should not be used by pregnant women, or people with asthma, diabetes, hypoglycemia, severe allergies, a slow heart rate, or low blood pressure.

Ergotamine tartrate generally is not used as a prophylactic migraine medication, as the sufferer should not take it daily because a dependency on the drug may develop. However, ergotamine tartrate in a very small dose can be used prophylactically. Bellergal is one such preventive medication that contains ergotamine, but in small enough amounts to be taken safely every day. It also contains phenobarbital and the antispasmodic belladonna. Side effects include drowsiness, blurred vision, and dryness of the mouth. Bellergal should not be used by pregnant women or people with glaucoma, high blood pressure, or coronary, liver, kidney, or arterial problems.

Some of the medications used prophylactically are antiserotonin substances that block the effect of serotonin on blood vessels. Serotonin is considered to be one of the chemicals causing the changes taking place during a migraine headache. There is thought to be a drop in the level of serotonin at the onset of a migraine attack. Methysergide maleate (Sansert) is one such medication. Methysergide has a constricting action on the scalp arteries, similar to serotonin. It also has a mild anti-inflammatory effect. About one-third of the people taking methysergide experience side effects such as aching or numbness, circulatory problems in the extremities, indigestion, nausea, vomiting, stomach cramps, or generalized edema when they first begin taking the medication. Insomnia, dizziness, and hallucinations can also occur, as well as an increase in appetite and weight gain. These symptoms eventually disappear in most patients. For those able to continue taking methysergide, the headaches can be reduced to at least half the frequency, and some people lose their headaches completely. Methysergide should be used primarily when a patient does not respond to other types of treatment. There are side effects associated with prolonged use, including kidney, heart, and liver problems. The effects are cumulative. Thus, patients taking this medication must stop it for a one- to two-month period for every six months of treatment. Methysergide should not be taken by pregnant women or people with coronary, circulatory, kidney, lung, or liver problems, or people with hypertension.

A milder medication which also works on serotonin is cyproheptadine (Periactin). It has an anthihistaminic as well as antiserotonin effect. Periactin is often used for children who suffer from migraine, as it does not have the side effects that Sansert does. It may cause drowsiness, a dry mouth, or increased appetite. Periactin should not be taken by pregnant women or people suffering from asthma, glaucoma, urinary or stomach problems. Anticonvulsant medications are also often used with younger migraine patients. In addition, they have been found to benefit those people whose electroencephalogram shows abnormal activity.

One drug that has been used experimentally in this country in the treatment of migraine headaches is clonidine (Catapres), a medication that has been used in the treatment of high blood pressure. It has been found to be effective in preventing migraine headaches. Clonidine is a beta-blocker which blocks the effect of adrenalin. Clonidine affects the blood vessels, making them less sensitive to the circulating vasoactive amines and, thus, less likely to dilate. It may lessen the severity and frequency of the headaches. Clonidine should not be taken by depressed patients.

Another drug used prophylactically for migraine headaches is phenelzine sulfate (Nardil). It is a monoamine oxidase (MAO) inhibitor used as a mood elevator in long-term depressions. It has also been found to be effective for patients with migraine problems that are very difficult to treat. Nardil can decrease the severity of the pain and the frequency of the headaches. There is a danger, however, that MAO inhibitors may induce a blood pressure crisis such as severe high or low blood pressure. Foods containing tyramine and alcoholic beverages can bring on this type of reaction and are absolutely forbidden for patients on this medication. Other medications such as cold remedies and many narcotics can lead to a low blood pressure crisis when a patient is taking Nardil. Thus, any person receiving a prescription for this medication must be carefully instructed to avoid these substances.

As depression, anxiety, and fatigue are three of the major provoking factors of migraine headaches, tranquilizers and/or antidepressants taken prophylactically can be extremely helpful in bringing the headache problem under control. Any form of treatment that decreases emotional reaction should also decrease the headache frequency. Stress is the most common precipitant of migraine headaches and cannot always be avoided. Thus, a mild sedative, either alone or contained in a prophylactic medication, may help the migraine sufferer. Tranquilizers aim to prevent the emotional situations that precipitate migraine headaches, but they should not be used too freely. It is better to determine the cause of the stress. Certain antidepressants, such as amitriptyline (Elavil), may prevent migraine headaches if taken daily. This has been found to be independent of any effect on the mood or depression of the sufferer. Tranquilizers and antidepressants must be taken for weeks or months to fully realize their effect on a headache problem.

Although a relationship between female hormones and migraine is believed to exist, various therapies involving different combinations and dosages of synthetic hormones, progesterones and estrogens, have not offered substantial relief of migraine headaches. Ergotamine tartrate may be given three days before and during the woman's menstrual period to help prevent menstrual migraine. Platelet inhibitors such as Persantine or Anturane are also utilized pre-menstrually in some patients. These medications inhibit the adherence of various materials and, thus, indirectly inhibit the release of certain vasoactive substances, especially serotonin. Fluid retention often occurs before the woman's menstrual period, and a diuretic taken daily for the week before the period starts is often helpful. Diuretics eliminate salt from the body and thus help to prevent the fluid retention that accompanies many migraine headaches. They can help to relieve some of the unpleasant associated symtpoms, but they do not prevent the migraine headaches. Also, phenothiazines may help the nausea and vomiting that accompany many migraine headaches.

Biofeedback

Biofeedback has proved effective in reducing both the frequency and severity of migraine headaches. It is a way of treating migraine without drugs. Medications can be misused, as some patients will take too much medication and this may lead to dependency. In addition, many medications have side effects so that many migraine headache patients are unable to take them.

Biofeedback is an active form of therapy on the part of the patient. A person's mind must be open to this type of treatment. Biofeedback is generally not a successful mode of therapy for people who are dependent on drugs. Younger patients usually are the best candidates for this type of therapy. With biofeedback training, a person learns to bring under conscious control certain bodily systems that he could not previously affect. It is possible to control one's blood pressure, heart rate, and hand temperature, to name but a few autonomic responses. It was previously thought that these functions were completely automatic and entirely involuntary. The autonomic nervous system can, however, be controlled.

Much of the responsibility for the control of headaches is delegated to the patient himself through biofeedback therapy. Patients must receive a certain amount of training in order to gain this control. During the training sessions electronic devices monitor the autonomic function and communicate to the individual the particular level of his autonomic system being monitored. The goal of the training program is for the patient to develop skills in order to control these autonomic systems without the feedback monitors. Regular practice, both with and without feedback monitors, is critical to success. Although there are individual differences, most patients can complete the training in about one month's time.

Biofeedback therapy used for controlling migraine headaches involves increasing the blood flow to the hands or "warming the hands" (see Figure 3). The mechanism behind this was accidentally discovered at the Menninger Clinic. An experiment was conducted to investigate the control of blood flow to the hands, having the subjects attempt to increase their hand temperatures. It was found that most of the patients were able to accomplish this. Coincidentally, one of the participants aborted an oncoming migraine headache while taking part in the experiment and increasing the blood flow to her hands. Further research was then conducted with more migraine sufferers, and the "hot hands" biofeedback technique was found to be a viable therapy for migraine headaches. It has been observed that the hands of many migraine sufferers are especially cold. Thinking about the hands becoming hot may increase their temperature and thus the blood flow to the hands. It is theorized that the increased blood flow to the hands comes from the head, lessening the head pain, as the blood vessels become less swollen.

Included in the temperature training session is the practice of certain relaxation exercises. These relaxation exercises alone can help to reduce the frequency of migraine headaches by lessening stress and fatigue, the two major precipitating factors of migraine headaches. Combining biofeedback with autogenic training is generally helpful. The autogenic phrases of Johannes Schultz focus on feelings of warmth and relaxtion. Autogenic training involves the individual's repeating various phrases, such as those below, to help him relax.

I feel quite quiet . . . I am beginning to feel quite relaxed. My feet feel heavy and relaxed . . . My ankles, my

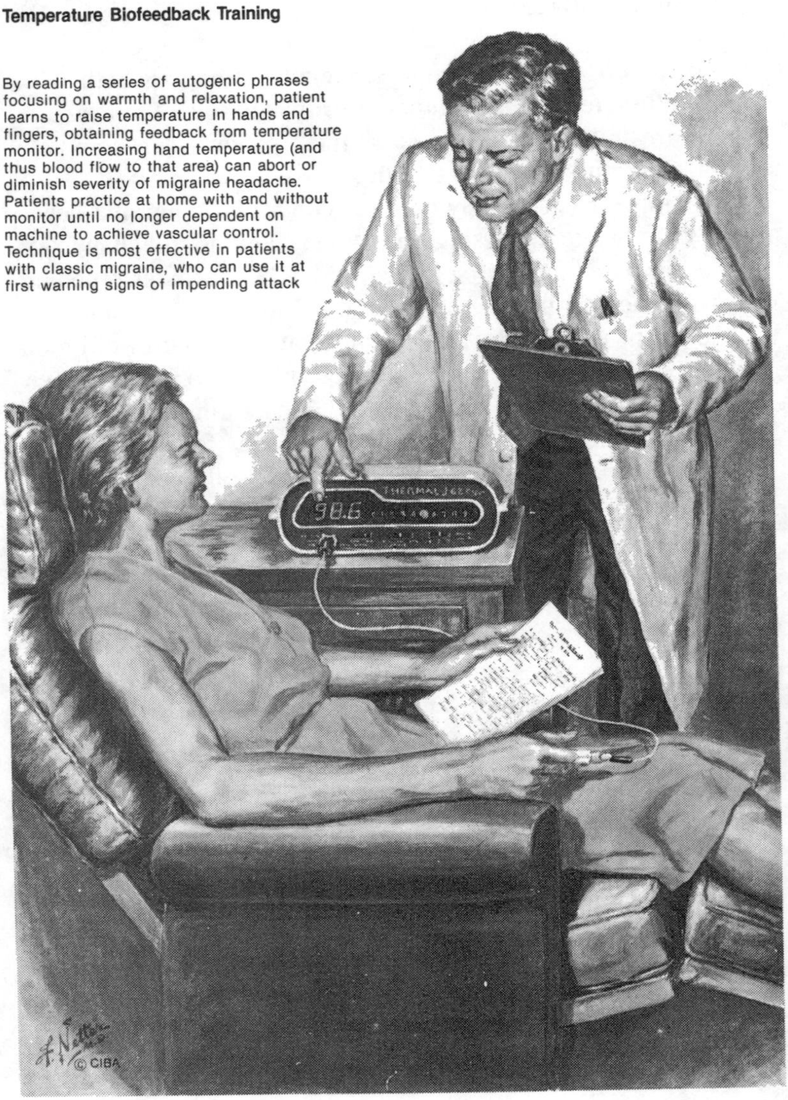

Temperature Biofeedback Training

By reading a series of autogenic phrases focusing on warmth and relaxation, patient learns to raise temperature in hands and fingers, obtaining feedback from temperature monitor. Increasing hand temperature (and thus blood flow to that area) can abort or diminish severity of migraine headache. Patients practice at home with and without monitor until no longer dependent on machine to achieve vascular control. Technique is most effective in patients with classic migraine, who can use it at first warning signs of impending attack

Figure 3
Reprinted by permission from *Clinical Symposia: CIBA*, Vol. 33, No. 2, 1981.

knees, and my hips feel heavy, relaxed, and comfortable . . . My solar plexus and the whole central portion of my body feel relaxed and quiet . . . My hands, my arms, and my shoulders feel heavy, relaxed, and comfortable . . . My neck, my jaws, and my forehead feel relaxed . . . They feel comfortable and smooth . . . My whole body feels quite heavy, comfortable, and relaxed. I am quite relaxed . . . My arms and hands are heavy and warm . . . I feel quite quiet . . . My whole body is relaxed and my hands are warm, relaxed and warm . . . My hands are warm . . . Warmth is flowing into my hands; they are warm . . . Warm.[1]

The relaxation exercises can help patients in biofeedback training to learn to raise their hand temperature as well. After practicing the relaxation exercises, patients try to warm their hands, often using visual imagery. Patients are encouraged to focus on warm and relaxing thoughts or mental images. Biofeedback training generally takes place in a dark, quiet, comfortable, and relaxing setting. During the training period, patients use a temperature monitor that indicates their hand temperature at the start and end of each session. A temperature sensor is placed on the finger and leads to the meter that registers the hand temperature. By using the monitor, the patient identifies the thoughts or images that will raise his hand temperature. Gradually, through practice, he can accomplish the increase without the use of the machine. The goal is to abandon the electronic device and raise one's hand temperature at will. The patient can then use his hand-warming ability abortively at the first sign of a headache.

Another type of biofeedback therapy is also used in treating migraine headaches. Since stress is such a common pre-

[1] Johannes H. Schultz and Wolfgang Luthe, "Autogenic Methods," in *Autogenic Therapy*, edited by Wolfgang Luthe (New York/London: Grune & Stratton, 1969).

cipitant of migraine headaches, electromyograph (EMG) feedback therapy is often found to be beneficial (see Figure 4). Electromyograph feedback can also be helpful to many migraine sufferers with muscle contraction headaches. The practice of progressive relaxation exercises such as the following, adapted from Joseph Wolpe's work, can help many patients accomplish total relaxation.

> Let all your muscles go loose and heavy. Just settle back quietly and comfortably. Wrinkle up your forehead now; wrinkle and smooth it out. Picture the entire forehead and scalp becoming smoother as the relaxation increases. Now, frown and crease your brows and study the tension. Let go of the tension again. Smooth out the forehead once more . . . Now, close your eyes tighter and tighter. Feel the tension . . . And relax your eyes. Keep your eyes closed gently, comfortably, and notice the relaxation . . . Now, clench your jaws, bite your teeth together; study the tension throughout the jaws . . . Relax your jaws now. Let your lips part slightly . . . Appreciate the relaxation . . . Now, press your tongue hard against the roof of your mouth. Look for the tension . . . All right. Let your tongue return to a comfortable and relaxed position . . . Now, purse your lips, press your lips together tighter and tighter . . . Relax the lips. Note the contrast between tension and relaxation. Feel the relaxation all over your face, all over your forehead and scalp, eyes, jaws, lips, tongue, and your neck muscles. Press your head back as far as it can go and feel the tension in the neck; roll it to the right and feel the tension shift; now, roll it to the left. Straighten your head and bring it forward and press your chin against your chest. Let your head return to a comfortable position, and study the relaxation. Let the relaxation develop . . . Shrug your shoulders right up. Hold the tension . . . Drop your shoulders and

Electromyographic Feedback Training

Relaxation of frontalis muscle is effective in reducing frequency of muscle contraction headache. Patient hears tone with pitch proportional to electromyographic level of muscle being monitored. As patient learns to reduce tension at one level, monitor can be reset to the next higher sensitivity. Office training sessions usually last 20 minutes; stereo headphones minimize distractions

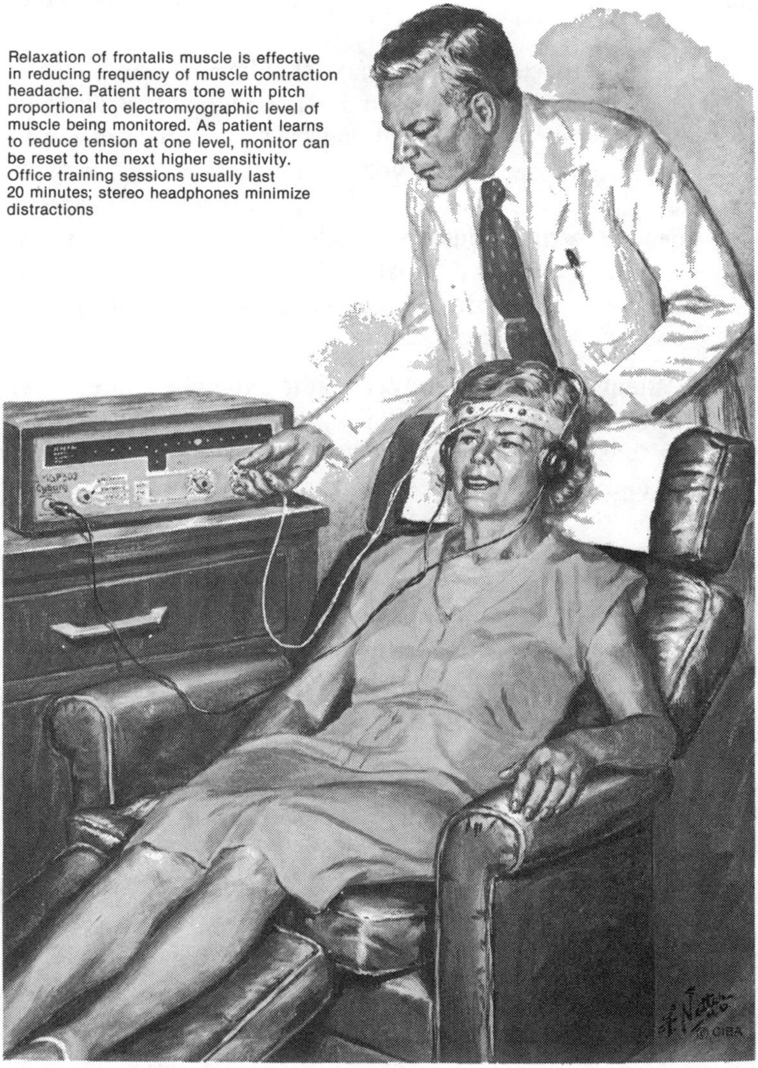

Figure 4
Reprinted by permission from *Clinical Symposia: CIBA*,
Vol. 33, No. 2, 1981.

feel the relaxation. Neck and shoulders relaxed. Shrug your shoulders again and move them around. Bring your shoulders up and forward and back. Feel the tension in your shoulders and in your upper back . . . Drop your shoulders once more and relax. Let the relaxation spread deep into the shoulders, right into your back muscles; relax your neck and throat, and your jaws and other facial areas as the pure relaxation takes over and grows deeper . . . Deeper . . . Even deeper.[2]

Patients are advised to focus on relaxing the entire body. During electromyograph feedback, electrodes which monitor muscle tension are placed across the forehead. The patient hears a tone, which changes in rate or pitch depending on his degree of muscle relaxation. Through electromyograph feedback patients are often able to identify their stress points, such as tightness in the forehead or brow, tension in the neck or shoulders, teeth grinding or jaw clenching. By practicing on the feedback monitor, the sufferer can find ways of reducing this tension, thus enabling him to relax during stressful periods or at the onset of a headache. Patients are trained to recognize when they are tensing their muscles too much and how to reduce this tension. Again, diligent practice of the techniques is very important. Electromyograph feedback often leads to a decrease in the severity and frequency of headaches in many patients.

[2] Joseph Wolpe, *The Practice of Behavior Therapy* (New York: Pergamon Press, 1969).

6

CLUSTER HEADACHES

Case History 10

S.M., aged 45, is a successful accountant who has always enjoyed good health. He is a former athlete but has exercised little in recent years and has gained 30 pounds in the last decade. He smokes heavily and on occasion drinks to excess. About two years ago he had a series of excruciating, usually nocturnal headaches, which began suddenly, lasted three weeks, and then ceased spontaneously. His physician was contacted at that time but offered no explanation for these episodes.

One month ago the nocturnal headaches started again. They often waken him at 3:00 A.M. and are localized to and above the left eye. The left eye waters copiously with the onset of headache. The left side of the nose is plugged initially and then runs later. His left eye becomes very red, perhaps because he rubs it. The pain is steady and intense, severe enough to make this stolid man cry for help. The pain usually lasts 45 minutes and then rapidly clears; thereafter, he feels perfectly well. He has noticed, however, that even small amounts of alcohol can reproduce this set of symptoms, and so he has stopped drinking completely in the last month.

His physician was contacted again and advised S.M. that he was working too hard and was too tense. He left for a week's vacation, but the headaches continued. He began to worry that he might have a brain tumor. In the last several days, however, the headaches have begun to disappear and are no longer so intense.

Cluster headaches are so named because of the characteristic grouping of the attacks. The headaches come in groups, or clusters, and the cause is unknown. This is one of the less common types of headache, vascular in nature, and brought on by cerebral dilatation. Some have considered cluster headache to be a type of migraine; today, most believe that it is an entirely different type of vascular headache. It is thought that histamine is released during a cluster attack. Also, it is possible for someone suffering from cluster headaches to suffer from migraine headaches as well.

The pain of cluster headache is generally very intense and severe and is often described as having a burning or piercing quality. It may be throbbing or constant. The scalp may be tender, and the arteries often can be felt increasing their pulsation. The pain is so intense that most sufferers cannot sit still during an attack and are often seen pacing during the acute phase. Cluster headaches generally reach their full force within five or ten minutes of their onset. The attacks are usually very similar, varying only slightly from one attack to the next.

Although the pain of a cluster headache comes on suddenly, a minimal type of warning of the oncoming headache may occur, including a feeling of discomfort or a mild, unilateral, burning sensation. The pain is of short duration, generally 30 to 45 minutes. It may, however, last anywhere from a few minutes to several hours. The headache then goes away, only to reoccur later in the day. Most sufferers get one to four headaches a day during a cluster period. They occur very regularly, generally at the same time each day. They have been called "alarm clock headaches."

Cluster headaches often awaken the sufferer in the early morning or during the night. The headache periods can last weeks or months and then go away completely for months or years. The cluster headache sufferer has a considerable amount of pain-free time between attacks. The clusters often occur in the spring or autumn. Due to their seasonal nature, cluster headaches are often mistakenly associated with allergies or business tensions. The seasons are, however, individual for each sufferer. In some people (about 20% of cluster headache sufferers), the attacks may be chronic. They are present all year round and do not come in groups. This makes the headaches more difficult to control.

The pain of a cluster headache is almost always unilateral, but it may change sides in different attacks. The pain is localized behind the eye or in the eye region. It may radiate to the forehead, temple, nose, cheek, or upper gum on the affected side. The affected eye may become swollen or droop. The pupil of the eye may contract. The nostril on the affected side of the headache is often congested. Excessive sweating may also occur, and the face may become flushed on the affected side. Cluster headaches are not associated with the gastrointestinal disturbances or photophobia found in other vascular headaches such as migraine.

Even small amounts of alcohol can precipitate attacks, as can other vasodilating substances such as nitroglycerin or histamine. Smoking can also increase the severity of cluster headaches. These substances will trigger headaches only during a cluster period. During this time the sufferer's blood vessels seem to change and are susceptible to the action of these vasoactive substances. The blood vessels are not sensitive to them at other times. Hormonal influences in women do not appear to be a factor in cluster headaches.

Cluster Profile

Cluster headaches are more common in men than women. Ninety percent of cluster headache sufferers are men. The headaches can occur at any age. There is not thought to be a familial incidence of cluster headaches, as with migraine headaches. Certain facial characteristics, however, are shared by many long-standing cluster headache sufferers. These include a furrowed brow; a ruddy complexion; pitted, coarse skin; a square, clefted chin; and a well-chiseled lower lip. The cluster headache victim often has a rugged, athletic build. Many have tiny veins showing on the nose or another part of the face. It has been found that many of the male cluster headache sufferers are heavy smokers. Peptic ulcers seem to be more frequent in the cluster headache sufferer, while there is a lesser number of angina pectoris attacks (recurrent chest pain) among these people. A graphic description of the typical cluster headache patient is presented in Figure 5.

Frank Capra, the famous director and producer, described his cluster headache as he was sitting in a hotel dining room:

> Suddenly a huge phantom bird sank three talons of its angry claws deeply into my head and face and tried to lift me. No warnings, no preliminary signs. Just wham! A massive, killing pain came over my right eye. I clutched my head, stumbled out to the broad lawns and over the hedges to the deserted tennis courts and then, there in the dark, I moaned, I panted. Ballooned my cheeks, blew out short bursts of air, licked my hot lips, wiped tears that poured out of my right eye, and clawed at my head trying to uproot the fiendish talons from their iron grip. One racking hour later the talons let go. The paroxysm eased as suddenly as it had convulsed. Euphoria set in. It's gone! Whopping headache, but it's gone! But that night, the monstrous bird sank vast ghostly talons into my head, the words welled up from deep within me; real; a soul

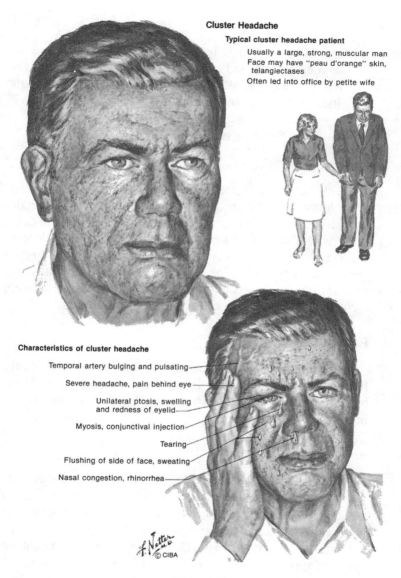

Cluster Headache

Typical cluster headache patient

Usually a large, strong, muscular man
Face may have "peau d'orange" skin, telangiectases
Often led into office by petite wife

Characteristics of cluster headache

Temporal artery bulging and pulsating

Severe headache, pain behind eye

Unilateral ptosis, swelling and redness of eyelid

Myosis, conjunctival injection

Tearing

Flushing of side of face, sweating

Nasal congestion, rhinorrhea

Figure 5
Reprinted by permission from *Clinical Symposia: CIBA*,
Vol. 33, No. 2, 1981.

cry. When prayer is for real, it hangs out the door latch
to your innards, and conscience pulls the latch, enters and
lets you have it. What was the pain all about? It is the
Judas pain; you welch, compromise; sell out.[1]

Treatment of Cluster Headache

General Measures

Psychological factors do not contribute to cluster headaches to the degree that they do with other vascular headaches
such as migraine. Thus, reducing stress or changing lifestyle
patterns will not help to prevent cluster headaches. Alcohol,
smoking, and nitrite-containing substances are known to trigger cluster headaches. Therefore, strict avoidance of alcohol,
smoking, and foods containing vasoactive substances during
a cluster period can reduce the incidence of attacks.

Relief of Attack

Most of the medications used in the treatment of cluster
headaches are also used in migraine headache treatment. These
medications are discussed in greater detail in the section on
migraine headache relief.

Abortive Therapy

It is difficult to treat cluster headaches abortively as there
is little or no warning before an attack. They may awaken a
person from sleep, reach their peak quickly, but then not last
long. Ergotamine tartrate will abort cluster headaches if it can
get into the bloodstream quickly enough to stop the blood
vessels from dilating. This is difficult with cluster headaches.
Ergotamine tartrate taken abortively should be in one of the

[1] Frank Capra, *The Name Above the Title* (New York: Macmillan,
1971).

forms that is absorbed into the bloodstream quickly, such as an injection or suppository. It may not abort the first headache of the day, the one that wakes the sufferer, but in large doses may reduce the ensuing daytime headaches. Because cluster headaches occur so predictably, taking ergotamine tartrate a few hours before the attack is expected may help to prevent the headache. Dihydroergotamine-45 (DHE-45) is a very fast-acting drug that is similar to ergotamine tartrate. It may begin to work as quickly as 15 to 60 seconds and is administered by injection. Due to its rapid entrance into the bloodstream, DHE-45 is often effective in aborting an oncoming cluster attack. Oxygen inhalation is another therapy that can be effective with cluster headaches. Oxygen will cause the blood vessels to constrict if inhaled at the beginning of a headache. Obviously, however, it is inconvenient for the sufferer to carry an oxygen tank around with him at all times. A powerful painkiller such as a narcotic may be used to dull the pain of an already-existing, out-of-control cluster headache. This should be used very infrequently, however, due to the addictive nature of narcotics.

Prophylactic Therapy

Generally the treatment of cluster headaches should be approached prophylactically. Medications that lessen vascular reactivity, inhibit vasoactive substances, or reduce inflammation can be effective in controlling cluster headaches. Methysergide maleate (Sansert) is often used in large doses to prevent cluster headaches. It must be used cautiously due to its side effects. Since methysergide maleate should not be taken for long periods of time, it is discontinued as soon as the group of headaches is over. Cyproheptadine (Periactin) is often used prophylactically for cluster headaches. Cyproheptadine is generally used for the chronic cluster headache sufferer, as prolonged use of methysergide maleate should be avoided.

Propranolol (Inderal) may also be taken daily to prevent cluster headaches. Its risks are not as great as those of methysergide. For very severe pain, corticosteroids are sometimes used. It is not known why they are effective, possibly because they reduce inflammation, or they may have an effect on the chemicals that cause cerebral dilation. Corticosteroids include dexamethasone (Decadron, Prednisone) and ACTH. ACTH is used in the treatment of arthritis and works on inflammation. It stems from the pituitary gland and stimulates the adrenal gland to produce cortisone. Steroids are used only when other medications have been ineffective, since they should not be used for any length of time. Indomethacin (Indocin) is another antiarthritic medication which has been found to be an effective treatment for cluster headaches. There is some evidence that the drug lithium may be an effective prophylactic treatment for some cluster headache sufferers, particularly those with chronic cluster headaches. Ergotamine tartrate may also be used as a prophylactic medication with cluster headaches. During an attack period, ergotamine tartrate may be taken two or three times a day to prevent the headaches from occurring. It must be discontinued if the group of headaches lasts too long, and its use must be closely monitored. Various surgical techniques have been attempted in the past to deal with cluster headaches. The head and neck nerves have been blocked or severed surgically, with unsuccessful results.

Many researchers believe that histamine, a powerful vasodilator, influences cluster headaches. The level of histamine in the individual's blood and urine increases during a cluster headache. This may cause the congested nostrils and watery eyes associated with cluster headache. Antihistamines, however, have not been found to be an effective form of therapy. Histamine desensitization is sometimes employed in preventing bouts of cluster headaches. The cluster headache sufferer's body gradually gets used to histamine until it is "desensitized," or no longer sensitive to it. In histamine desensitization a patient receives small amounts of histamine intravenously by a slow drip for 21 straight days. The amount of histamine given is gradually increased from day to day. Too much histamine will provoke a cluster headache. It is a time-consuming type of therapy, involving at least two hours each day. It is difficult to evaluate the usefulness of histamine desensitization; it has been found to be effective for some cluster headache victims but not for others. For some people, histamine desensitization may decrease the intensity of the cluster headaches and shorten the duration of the group of headaches. It may also increase the length of the interval between cluster periods.

7

MUSCLE CONTRACTION HEADACHES

Case History 11

J.M., aged 49, has complained of headaches for 20 years. They occur almost daily. They are not well localized but are often described as a band of pain about the forehead which waxes and wanes. Sometimes he notes pain in the neck and lower part of the head. He takes large quantities of over-the-counter medications, switching from one to another. By his own admission, he is an aspirin popper. He has been to many physicians and has been subjected to examinations and testing, but no cause for these headaches has been found. In addition to headache, he describes chronic fatigue, which is not relieved by rest. Indeed, he sleeps poorly, has problems getting to sleep, and often wakes early in the morning. He often has a vague sense of being unwell. He has withdrawn from many social activities; they tire him and are too much trouble besides. He would rather stay at home now. He has noted a decrease in libido. He is irritable, has trouble concentrating, and has a "short fuse." He feels that he

106

is more emotional than previously, feeling at times that he might weep without reason.

He recently reported to his physician, and another unsuccessful neurological survey was done. His physician wisely referred J.M. to a clinical psychologist for psychological testing. This revealed a marked masked depression, expressed particularly as body complaints. J.M. continues to consume rather large quantities of aspirin regularly.

Muscle contraction headaches are the most prevalent type of headache. They are generally bilateral, surrounding or forming a band around the head, with a dull, aching pain that lasts days, months, or years. Stiffness is often felt in the neck; the pain originates in the muscles, and the muscles can often be felt contracting. The headaches strike frequently or become almost continuous, present all the time. An accompanying sleep disturbance is characteristic of muscle contraction headaches. Peak times for the headaches are early morning and early evening. They generally become more frequent on weekends and holidays. Both sexes are affected by muscle contraction headaches, but women sufferers outnumber men. Women may seem to predominate because they tend to seek medical help more readily. Muscle contraction headaches can also occur in the migraineur. However, they do not appear to have the hereditary component of migraine headaches. Muscle contraction headaches usually begin in adulthood. A patient will often ascribe the headache to some minor illness or injury in the past. It is generally trivial and could not really have a bearing on the headache problem. There is no identifiable cause of muscle contraction headaches. Nor has any specific personality been identified. The muscle contraction headache sufferer is likely to appear outwardly calm and relaxed, with a seemingly expressionless face. There is an internalized feeling of helplessness. Muscle contraction headache victims are often overly concerned with their own abilities in performing or coping.

Aggravating Factors

Case History 12

M.H. is a homemaker, aged 39, who enjoys good health, with the exception of incapacitating headaches. She has a very neat house, with everything in its place, and always finishes her housework and other projects. One-sided headaches started at age 18. They were diagnosed as migraine and were helped by the use of Ergomar tablets PRN. These migraine-type headaches occurred almost once a week and lasted two to three days, accompanied by an aura of flashing lights about a half-hour before the headache.

The patient reports that she also has severe headaches with her periods. When the headache is severe, she experiences nausea and vomiting and occasionally sees black spots before her eyes. She also notes that chocolate brings on headaches, and remembers that her grandmother had headaches.

Three years ago, M.H. started having another type of headache, which was present on both sides of her head and included the cervical spine. Upon questioning, M.H. reveals that she and her husband have been having marital problems for the past four years. This second type of headache is always present upon awakening. She has difficulty falling asleep but always wakes up early in the morning, usually by 4:30 or 5:00 A.M. M.H. feels depressed because of the headaches. She states that she has lost interest in her home and children. She tries to sleep to escape, and usually feels fatigued. She says she cannot tolerate the pain much longer as it lasts all day and sometimes into the night.

There is usually an emotional trigger behind muscle contraction headaches. Although there may be other precipitating factors with these headaches, one can generally find an emotional component when they become a chronic problem. Emotional factors that can cause muscle contraction headaches include depression, chronic anxiety, stress, suppressed anger, worry, frustration, and fear. The depression is often of such depth that the sufferer does not even know that he is depressed. He thinks that this is the way life is to be lived and therefore associates the accompanying headaches with some past illness or injury.

Headaches associated with depression establish a regular pattern, occurring primarily in the early morning and early evening. The most common causes of depression are related to job conflicts and family relationships. The depression itself can be disabling. It varies in intensity. Depression can cause a slowing down of all of one's functions, or it can take the form of agitation. A depressed headache patient will have many accompanying emotional and physical complaints. He often has difficulty concentrating or remembering things, loses interest easily, and cannot make decisions. Fatigue, weakness, irritability, and suicidal feelings are sometimes present, as well as a decrease in sexual activity. The depressed headache sufferer generally exhibits a sleep disturbance such as early waking or frequent waking throughout the night. Other symptoms of depression include stomach problems, constipation, loss of weight, or lack of appetite. Depressed patients complain of feeling sad and often burst into tears. They may be introverted and dwell on their illness. A post-traumatic headache is usually put into this category, as it follows an injury to the head, although there may be no organic cause for the headache. The patient becomes depressed, and it is the depression that causes the post-traumatic headache.

Muscle contraction headaches may also be caused by anxiety. These headaches occur unpredictably, at almost any time of day. Headaches associated with anxiety usually involve insomnia as a symptom, with the sufferer having difficulty falling asleep. Added stress also plays a large role in aggravating the muscle contraction headache. Stress can lead to a tightening of the muscles, resulting in head pain.

The muscle contraction headache can be caused by poor posture, close work under poor lighting conditions, or cramps from assuming an unnatural head position or rigid neck position for long periods of time. Arthritis, primarily cervical arthritis, can also provoke muscle contraction headaches, as well as pain from other places such as the neck, eyes, and teeth. Disturbances in the neck muscles, bones, or discs can precipitate muscle contraction headaches, as can abnormal conditions in facial organs. Eyestrain caused by one eye trying to compensate for a weakness in the other eye's muscles can provoke a muscle contraction headache. Faulty alignment of the teeth, leading to teeth grinding or jaw clenching, can also cause head pain. These abnormalities make it more likely that the muscles in the area will contract, thus initiating the headache. For some people, muscle contraction alone provokes the headache. Outside factors such as noise and lights can also aggravate a muscle contraction headache.

Treatment

Chronic muscle contraction headache sufferers should seek medical help. Generally one does not have to be concerned about the occasional "tension" headache. It can usually be relieved by simple analgesics such as aspirin or acetaminophen. The occasional tension headache is generally associated with temporary stressful situations and fatigue. When the headaches occur as frequently as a few times a month or every day, however, they warrant medical intervention. The presence of a muscle contraction headache may be symptomatic of some other disease causing the contraction of the muscles. Thus, it must be thoroughly checked. The pain of chronic muscle contraction headaches does not usually respond to simple analgesics, while the pain of episodic muscle contraction headaches usually does.

A multifaceted approach is needed in the treatment of muscle contraction headaches, since there are numerous causes and provoking factors. It is necessary to treat the head pain symptom as well as trying to find the root of the problem. Certain forms of psychological, physical, pharmacological, or biofeedback therapy may be employed in muscle contraction headache treatment. Different types of therapy are often combined in order to bring the head pain under control. Occasionally, one type of therapy will replace another type because of the side effects or negative results experienced from the first type. One type of therapy may be beneficial for one individual, while another form will be more successful for another person.

Psychological Approaches

Since emotional factors so often play a role in muscle contraction headaches, the physician must explore the sufferer's marital, social, and occupational relationships, along with his personality traits and ways of handling stress. It is necessary to determine which elements in the sufferer's life provoke the headaches. It must be emphasized to the patient that it is important to find any emotional triggers for the headaches in order to seek a long-term solution to the headache problem, and not just temporary treatment of the symptoms. Isolating stress factors is difficult, as the sufferer is not always aware of them. Allowing him to talk about his life, including his work and family, may help to identify the cause. The headache sufferer and physician must have a good, trusting relationship. Psychotherapy may be helpful for some sufferers, but this does not necessarily indicate the presence of a severe emotional disturbance. It may, however, facilitate discovering the individual's emotional triggers. The psychotherapy required may be of short duration. The muscle contraction headache sufferer needs reassurance and patience. Efforts to reduce emotional stress, and occasionally reorganizing one's life, may be helpful in bringing the headache problem under control.

The appropriate psychological management of patients with muscle contraction headaches caused by depression or anxiety is important. It may take time and a number of office visits to discover the cause of a depression or anxiety headache. Again, it is important to find the root of the problem, rather than just treating the symptom. Some physicians will treat the headache and others will treat the depression, but one must realize that the headache is part of the depression, and it should be treated as such. For many sufferers, trying to relieve the depression will also alleviate the painful headache symptom. However, some individuals' depressions are caused by the pain, and by relieving the pain, the depression will often be relieved. If the depression is very severe, psychiatric treatment may be necessary. A chronic muscle contraction headache sufferer is likely to be in pain nearly every day, with an accompanying effect on the emotions. A circular phenomenon is often set in motion, in which pain provokes emotional upset which provokes more pain, provoking emotional upset, etc. Treatment will necessitate interrupting this cycle.

Physical Approaches

Cervical collars, which support the neck and help the individual maintain good posture, may help in bringing the muscle contraction headache problem under control. Avoiding situations or conditions that involve distortion or rigidity of posture can also help to alleviate some muscle contraction headaches. Many sufferers have found careful exercise and massage of the neck muscles effective. Exercises should include those specifically aimed at relaxing tight muscles. Heat applied to the neck area may also be helpful, as heat is a muscle relaxant.

Pharmacological Approaches

Pharmacological treatment of muscle contraction headaches should generally be considered a temporary solution to help bring the headache problem quickly under control. In the meantime, effort should be directed at isolating any emotional triggers. The goal of treatment is to slowly decrease and phase out medication. There are two types of mood-altering drugs used in the treatment of muscle contraction headaches: antidepressants, which raise one's spirits, and tranquilizers, which reduce tension and anxiety. Antidepressants and tranquilizers enable headache sufferers to more easily tolerate and function with their pain.

A depression can be attacked chemically with medication, without even determining the cause. During a depressive headache there is a significant decrease in catecholamines, a group of chemicals that includes norepinephrine and dopamine. The use of medication that increases the catecholamines in the brain can help to control this type of headache. An antidepressant is the drug of choice if depression is present with the headache. Treatment of the depression may be the key to bringing many chronic headache problems under control. Antidepressants are used preventively in the treatment of muscle contraction headaches, as they have no effect on an already-existing headache.

Two types of antidepressants are used: tricyclic antidepressants and monoamine oxidase (MAO) inhibitors. Tricyclic antidepressants help to preserve catecholamines in the brain. They include the following hydrochloride medications: amitriptyline (Elavil), protriptyline (Vivactil), nortriptyline (Aventyl), imipramine (Tofranil), desipramine (Pertofrane), and doxepin (Sinequan). Tricyclic antidepressants may be prescribed in combination with each other. One may be prescribed for the depressive headache while another may be added to relieve the sleep disturbance associated with depression. This will help the sufferer sleep through the night. Tricyclic antidepressants may take several weeks to show their effectiveness. Some of the possible side effects include drowsiness, dryness of the mouth, tingling fingers, and blurred vision. Changes in pulse, heart rhythm, blood pressure, and behavior may also occur. Tricyclic antidepressants occasionally lose their effectiveness after a few years, and the headaches begin again.

MAO inhibitors, another type of antidepressant medication, are mood elevators that slow down the metabolism of catecholamines, thus preserving them. It is suspected that both MAO inhibitors and tricyclic antidepressants may not only relieve the depression but may also raise the pain threshold. As with migraine headache sufferers on these drugs, muscle contraction headache patients taking MAO inhibitors must be very careful to avoid foods containing tyramine and all alcoholic beverages since a blood pressure crisis may arise.

The anxiety headache is generally treated with tranquilizing drugs and mild pain relievers. Tranquilizers are usually used prophylactically to prevent muscle contraction headaches. They will not abort an already-existing headache, although they may help the sufferer relax. Tranquilizers may aid in counteracting the tension that provokes many muscle contraction headaches. They are thought to raise the sufferer's pain threshold and lessen his reactivity to stress. Only some of the milder types of tranquilizers are used in the treatment of muscle contraction headaches. They include chlordiazepoxide (Librium), diazepam (Valium), chlorazepate (Tranxene), meprobamate (Equanil, Miltown), phenobarbital, hydroxyzine (Atarax, Vistaril), and oxazepam (Serax). Some of the side effects include drowsiness, lack of coordination, and depression. Alcohol should not be consumed in combination with any of the above medications. Tranquilizers should be used carefully and only for short periods of time because of their habituating nature. There can be withdrawal symptoms if, after prolonged use at high doses, tranquilizers are stopped abruptly.

Medications known as muscle relaxants are also used in the treatment of muscle contraction headaches. They are often used in combination with other medications. Muscle relaxants may relieve the muscle spasms that are the product of excessive contraction of the scalp, face, and neck muscles, thus helping to control the ensuing muscle contraction headache. Stronger analgesics may be prescribed as painkillers, and sedatives may be prescribed when there is a sleep disturbance accompanying the headache. Barbiturates and narcotics are prescribed only in extreme instances and with extreme caution. They are basically sedatives that reduce anxiety, pain, and one's reaction to pain, but they are habituating and must not be taken with alcohol. They include amobarbital (Amytal), butabarbital (Butisol), pentobarbital (Nembutal), phenobarbital (Luminal), and secobarbital (Seconal). Some are combined with analgesics, such as Fiorinal. Because of the complex nature of many muscle contraction headache problems, it is sometimes necessary to use combinations of analgesics, muscle relaxants, antidepressants, and tranquilizers in their treatment.

Biofeedback

There have been significant results in using relaxation and biofeedback techniques to treat recurring muscle contraction headaches. Many muscle contraction headache sufferers are unable to relax; therefore, relaxation therapy may be helpful. Relaxation exercises and biofeedback are ways of controlling the headache problem for some people without using medication. With biofeedback, the individual is able to control bodily systems that were previously thought to be involuntary. The patient is integrally involved in his own treatment. With muscle contraction headaches, the sufferer wants to gain control over the neck, face, and scalp muscles and be able to relax them at will. In relaxation training the sufferer practices relaxing each muscle group individually and progressively until he is totally relaxed. Progressive relaxation exercises adapted from the work of Joseph Wolpe can help the patient to achieve maximum relaxation (see the biofeedback section in Chapter 5 on Migraine Headaches). These are usually practiced at the beginning of biofeedback training. The biofeedback training sessions take place in a quiet, dimly lit room with the patient sitting or reclining in a comfortable chair.

The type of biofeedback predominantly used with muscle contraction headaches is electromyograph (EMG) feedback. Electromyograph feedback is based on the research of Drs. Budzynski, Stoyva, and Adler of the University of Colorado. Electrodes are placed across the forehead on the skin over the frontalis muscle. They record the electrical activity of the muscles as they contract. At the other end, the electrodes are attached to an electronic monitor. A sound is fed back to the individual at a pitch or rate directly related to the degree of relaxation in the muscles; thus, the tension in the frontalis muscle is converted into sound. Usually when the frontalis muscle relaxes so do the scalp, neck, and upper body muscles. The patient controls the sound by gaining control over the tension in his muscles. Muscle contraction leads to an increase in the feedback tone while muscle relaxation is reinforced by a diminishing of the tone. The individual practices various relaxation techniques while being monitored by the electromyograph machine and thus tries to discover ways to reduce the feedback sound. While hooked up to the electromyograph monitor, the patient is advised to experiment with various thoughts and positions until he achieves maximum relaxation. Each individual, when attached to the feedback monitor, learns to identify his particular tensor points in the face, neck, and shoulder areas. Tensor or stress points often identified include neck tension, tightening of the shoulders, teeth grinding, jaw clenching, and tightening and wrinkling of the forehead. As the patient is able to relax these muscles, he will often gain control of his muscle contraction headache problem.

During a muscle contraction headache, the face, scalp, and neck muscles are overcontracting, and the sufferer must become aware of this. The goal is to recognize when muscles are contracting and be able to relax tight muscles without the feedback monitor. Frequent practice of the relaxation exercises that the individual has found useful in reducing his muscle tension is necessary for control of the head pain. While regular practice can prevent many headaches from occurring, the relaxation exercises should also be used at the first signs of a headache.

For many muscle contraction headache sufferers, relaxation and electromyograph feedback training have led to a significant reduction in headache frequency and severity. Biofeedback may be helpful to some sufferers from depressive headaches; however, the concomitant use of antidepressant medication may be necessary.

8

HEADACHES IN CHILDREN

Headaches in children can be caused by a wide range of factors including fever, eyestrain, measles, mumps, inner-ear infections, motion sickness, or anxiety. They may also be the result of imitative behavior if the child's parents suffer from headaches. Headaches in children can be classified into the same types as those of adults: vascular, muscle contraction, traction, and inflammatory. The physician must initially formulate a correct diagnosis in treating a child sufferer. The head should be carefully measured and a complete neurological workup with tests, including skull x-rays, electroencephalogram, and blood work, should be done. The goal is to control the headache problem while the sufferer is young in order to prevent the headaches from becoming a lifelong problem. Discovering the cause is vital. As with adult cephalalgia victims, it is necessary to determine any headache triggers and try to eliminate them. The parents usually play a significant role in controlling the child's headache problem.

Some of the same medications used to treat adult headache problems are also utilized with children, but usually in smaller dosages and in different combinations. Generally, only the milder medications are prescribed. Simple analgesics may be helpful for the child sufferer, or a mild sedative may be effective. Narcotics should never be given to children, as they are too potent and can easily lead to habituation. The child must be able to take his medication at the first sign of a headache; thus, the child's teacher and school must be made aware of the problem and the physician's recommended treatment. The teacher and school nurse will need to cooperate by allowing the child to follow his prescription.

Approximately one-third of all migraine sufferers experience the onset of their headaches before the age of 10. The symptoms of migraine are often different in the young cephalgic and may include listlessness, painful sensitivity to light, or fever. The child may experience motion sickness, recurring episodes of nausea and vomiting, and/or unexplained abdominal pain, which often develops into a more typical migraine headache pattern later in life. It is thought that the biliousness and colic found in some children may be early migraine symptoms. These incomplete attacks are referred to as "migraine variants" and may be totally void of head pain. Vascular headaches in children may be classical in nature with an accompanying aura and one-sided pain; however, childhood migraine usually affects both sides of the head. Child victims often experience more frequent attacks which are shorter in duration than those of adults. In some instances, the childhood migraine does not persist into adulthood. A history of migraine is usually found in the family of the childhood sufferer. Cephalgic children may exhibit many of the same personality traits as adult sufferers: anxiety, tension, and compulsive perfectionism. Migraine headaches in children have many of the same causes and precipitating factors as those in adults, such as diet, hunger, fatigue, and a change in routine. They are frequently precipitated by stressful or exciting events. Cyproheptadine (Periactin) is often used prophylactically for the child migraine sufferer, with very small doses of ergotamine tartrate or isometheptene mucate (Midrin) to abort immediate headaches. Propranolol has also been found to be a good preventive medication. Methysergide and ergotamine tartrate are generally not used prophylactically with childhood migraine. Slight abnormalities are sometimes found in the electroencephalogram of children with migraine. Anticonvulsant medications such as Dilantin are also used occasionally to effectively treat childhood migraine sufferers.

Muscle contraction headaches are common in children. As with adult muscle contraction headaches, the pain surrounds the head or forms a band around it, and may involve neck tenderness and muscle spasms. These headaches are often related to stress in family or school situations. Medication is not always needed in the treatment of childhood muscle contraction headaches. Minimizing or eliminating emotional stress may be all that is needed to bring the headache problem under control. In children, simple analgesics often relieve the pain. With depressive headaches, tricyclic antidepressants such as amitriptyline (Elavil) may be effective.

Traction and inflammatory headaches also occur in children. If they involve fever, meningitis or encephalitis should be ruled out as a causative factor. Tumors in children have similar symptoms to those found in adults, with the pain present upon awakening, increasing with movement, becoming progressively more severe, and presenting accompanying neurological signs. Tumors, however, are an infrequent cause of headaches in children.

9

HEADACHES IN THE ELDERLY

At 50 years, 'tis said, afflicted citizens lose their sick headaches.
—Ralph Waldo Emerson, "Old Age," *Society and Solitude*

Migraine headaches are usually not found in elderly people. They generally subside after middle age, although the accompanying aura may remain. Migraine headaches rarely begin in later life. If a headache with migraine-type characteristics appears for the first time in an elderly person, it may be a symptom of a more serious vascular disorder and should be thoroughly checked.

Temporal arteritis most often occurs in people over 50 years of age. When an elderly person complains of a headache problem for the first time, temporal arteritis should be considered. This condition involves an inflammation of the temporal artery, with the artery becoming swollen and tender as the blood flow through it is blocked. The scalp blood vessels are generally affected first, but the cerebral vessels may also become inflamed. The headache that sometimes accompanies temporal arteritis is very severe, one-sided, and of a persistent, deep, aching or burning, throbbing quality. The burning sen-

121

sation helps to distinguish this type of headache from others. Lying horizontally generally increases the pain. Other symptoms include pain with chewing, pain in the teeth or jaw, and facial swelling or redness. Sufferers of temporal arteritis may also experience a lack of appetite, weakness, joint and muscle pain throughout the body, fever, anxiety, depression, and a general feeling of sickness. Many patients experience partial or even complete loss of vision in one eye. Thus, it is important to begin treatment before the inflammation spreads to intracranial arteries. Immediate treatment is necessary to prevent permanent loss of vision or stroke. Steroids (cortisone-type medications) are often used in the treatment of temporal arteritis. They reduce the inflammation, permitting the blood to flow freely and relieving the head pain. Treatment should last at least a year, although the headache may end after a few months if properly treated. A test that measures the sedimentation rate of the blood will help confirm the diagnosis of temporal arteritis.

Herpes zoster, or shingles, usually affects older people. Herpes can occur at any site on the body, and usually follows the course of a sensory nerve (a nerve that transmits sensation to the spinal cord). The pain of shingles may remain after the acute manifestations of herpes zoster have disappeared. The resultant pain is of a stabbing nature, with constant burning features. In some cases, the nerve damage is so great that there is loss of sensation over the entire area, and a definite anesthesia exists.

Although shingles can occur anywhere on the body, it is most commonly seen over the distribution of the fifth cranial nerve, which supplies sensory perception to the face and head. The division of the nerve that supplies sensation around the eye and cornea is particularly affected. During the acute viral infection, there is a small blisterlike rash which rarely crosses the midline. This occurrence is so typical that it enables quick diagnosis of the problem.

Certain trophic changes in the skin following shingles have been observed. These include a lack of vitality to the skin and blanching of the skin, which tends to distinguish it in color from the unaffected area. If the pain persists after the acute infection, transcutaneous stimulation over the area may be of help. Other methods of treatment include massage and injections of hydrocortisone into the area. Most treatments, however, have disappointing results. Although radical neurosurgery has been performed, it is not always recommended. The combination of a tricyclic antidepressant with a phenothiazine tranquilizer has been found to be successful in many intractable cases.

Trigeminal neuralgia (tic douloureux) also generally strikes people over age 50. The head pain is unilateral, very intense, and recurrent, affecting the facial region. It is an aching, burning type of pain, often set off by touch, chewing, laughing, talking, or even a cold breeze. The pain is intermittent, with jabs lasting for approximately 30 seconds, followed by a few pain-free moments, and then another painful jab, and so on, lasting for a few hours at a time. The attacks can go on for weeks or months. Anticonvulsant medications may reduce the sensitivity in the facial region, thus relieving the pain. They may take effect anywhere from a few hours to a day after initiating treatment, and therapy should continue for weeks or months. Carbamazepine is one such anticonvulsant drug. Other medications that may be tried if carbamazepine is not successful include diphenylhydantoin and chlorphenesin. If none of these three medications is effective, surgery may be indicated.

10

POST-TRAUMATIC HEADACHES

There are various types of post-traumatic headaches, each related to the part of the head that is injured and to the alterations to the nerves and the blood vessels that occur at the time of the injury. Short, throbbing pain in a localized area usually indicates that an artery has been affected. Organ damage is signaled when physical effort brings pain. Common whiplash pain results from the strain of head and neck muscles. Injury to a nerve is felt in the soft tissue around the nerve fiber. Most headaches due to such injuries disappear within three to six months. A family history of migraine and the psychological makeup of the patient, however, can influence the headache's duration.

Concussion, or loss of consciousness after a head injury, will often result in a headache after consciousness is regained. One must be concerned if the headache becomes progressively worse or is accompanied by drowsiness. This may be caused by a hemorrhage developing between the skull bone and the dura, or under the dural membrane, which lines it. The expansion of the hemorrhage compresses the brain and displaces blood vessels. The clot must be removed by a neurosurgeon so that the pressure may be eased. This condition may even arise long after the original injury if the hemorrhage is slow-growing.

Whiplash injury is a word picture of the process that takes place when the body remains stable as the head receives a jolt. The result is a sore neck and pain in the back of the head. Although the symptoms usually disappear in a few days, there have been myriad cases where they persist. Neurotic or hysterical reactions complicate this syndrome.

Dr. Harold G. Wolff, the famous headache researcher from Cornell University, has divided post-traumatic headache into three primary groups. The first group resembles muscle contraction or tension headache. The second is caused by scar tissue from the injury. And the third is a vascular headache, like migraine: one-sided, with nausea, vomiting, and swelling of the arteries of the scalp. Any injury to the scalp arteries makes them more susceptible to the painful dilatation that results in post-traumatic migraine, with the pain limited to the area of injury. There may also be a jabbing type of pain if the scar tissue involves nerves. Treatment is the same as for migraine, although surgery to tie off and cut the affected nerve or artery may be necessary in extreme cases. Anticonvulsant drugs are also used.

Further work by Dr. Wolff concerns the patient with muscle contraction headache after injury. He found that in three-fourths of those injured the muscles were continuously active throughout the headache and that the activity was greatest at the site of the headache. Although the activity may not have been the causative agent, it must be considered as a factor since mental and physical relaxation is necessary to lessen or eliminate headache. This type of headache is a dull, continuous pressure or tightness in the head. It intensifies with vascular dilatation and is accompanied by anxiety and depression.

There are often legal arguments about the existence of post-traumatic headache. However, headache experts do see headache resembling migraine occurring after injury. Another type of vascular headache which is prevalent only after exertion can also be ascribed to trauma. Excessive forces on the head and neck muscles can produce a post-traumatic headache that resembles muscle contraction headache.

Many patients with frequent headaches fear that their headaches make them more prone to stroke. This fear, of course, increases as the patient grows older. A person suffering from long-standing migraine, however, does not have any greater tendency toward stroke than the normal population. In rare instances, a severe migraine attack leaves some residual damage reminiscent of a stroke. Sometimes a physician will have difficulty differentiating a migraine that begins later in life from early stroke symptoms.

The two main types of stroke occur when a blood vessel to the brain bleeds (a cerebral hemorrhage), or when a blood vessel is blocked (a cerebral infarction). Cerebral hemorrhage patients almost always suffer from headache, especially if blood enters the area surrounding the brain, displacing pain-sensitive blood vessels. The pain is sudden, severe, and persistent.

11
LIFE-THREATENING CAUSES OF HEADACHE

The question most frequently posed to the headache specialist by other doctors is: "How does one guard against missing a brain tumor in a headache patient?" It is a serious concern. Brain tumors often present headache as one of their symptoms and can be confused with migraines and other headaches. However, a brain tumor is just one of several disorders with life-threatening or disabling consequences for which headache is often a presenting complaint.

Before discussing catastrophic headaches, it should be emphasized that only a small proportion of headaches actually have organic causes or are life-threatening. It has been estimated that only 2% of headache sufferers are represented in this group. Yet it is a basic fear of all chronic headache patients that they have a life-threatening disease, and it is important that the physician complete a thorough history and neurological examination and order necessary tests to rule out these catastrophic causes. No matter what the cause of the headache, each patient requires a thorough history, as discussed in Chapter 4, and a complete neurological examination that tests mental status, cerebellar function, peripheral nerves, cranial nerves, motor and sensory functions, and reflexes.

One primary clue to an organic cause is recent onset of headache. This does not include the patient with a long history of the same type of headache recurring month after month or year after year. The patient who gets a headache for the first time deserves a thorough workup.

The headache of *brain tumor* is usually of recent onset. It is characterized by a pattern of progressive worsening in a short period of time. It may become increasingly unbearable after a change in posture, such as standing up after sitting. Another clue is an increase in the headache with exertion, although this also occurs with migraine. At the onset, the brain tumor headache may be mild and easily relieved by analgesics. Although headache may be the primary sign of a brain tumor, the associated symptoms will usually confirm the diagnosis. If the patient exhibits loss of memory, disorientation, difficulty in making judgments, visual changes, or has seizures accompanying his headaches for the first time, one should be suspicious of an expanding lesion such as a brain tumor. The doctor who examines this patient neurologically should be cognizant of numbness in one hand or leg, weakness in an arm or leg, and speech or memory disorders. A brain tumor can occur at any age. If he suspects a brain tumor, the physician should do a CAT scan as part of his initial workup.

A condition similar to a brain tumor is a *brain abscess*. The condition is progressive, as in brain tumor. If a person has any type of heart valve lesion or a lesion in the large blood vessels leading to the brain which could produce an embolus, one should be suspicious of a brain abscess. Infections of the middle ear or teeth also point to a brain abscess. However, the patient with a brain abscess will show signs of fever along with increased intracranial pressure, which can be confirmed by observing the optic nerve as it enters the eye, and by definite neurological changes. Sometimes the person will complain of a stiff neck, which can be indicative of an infection.

A *subdural hematoma*, a clot beneath the covering of the brain, can start in a nagging manner and gradually increase in intensity. It is usually associated with a clouding of consciousness, and the patient appears dull and not alert. The family physician is more apt to diagnose this condition rather than the specialist since he knows the baseline of the patient's normal status and alertness. The neurological examination by the physician will reveal some disturbance in sensation and arm or leg strength, which will become progressively worse. The physician examining the patient should obtain a history of head injury in these cases. The trauma is obvious in younger people with subdural hematoma but difficult to detect in older patients, who often do not remember a minor traumatic event, such as bumping one's head while getting out of a car. Older patients who are on anticoagulant drugs for either heart disease or strokes, who have diabetes or blood disturbances, or who drink excessive quantities of alcohol are more prone to develop a subdural hematoma.

There is a type of head injury above the linings of the brain known as *epidural hematoma*. The headache is sudden, severe, increasing, and unbearable. There is always a history of injury. The person may be lucid for a short period of time and within 24 hours progressively fall into stupor and then coma. As with subdural hematoma, the headache is associated with clouding of consciousness. The patient with this condition is usually elderly and sometimes an alcoholic. This is a neurosurgical emergency and needs rapid management to remove the blood clot and guard against permanent injury or death.

If a patient in his fifties or sixties develops migraine-like headache symptoms for the first time, *transient ischemic attacks* are a possibility. TIA may be a warning of an impending stroke. Migraine rarely starts after the age of 40; thus, one should consider organic causes for patients with late-onset headaches. Headache can be an important symptom and occurs in about 25–30% of patients with this condition. Usually the carotid artery is diseased, and the attacks are located on the same side as the affected carotid. The headache attacks occur episodically as in migraine, but the headache is usually not as severe as migraine. If the physician examines the neck with a stethoscope, he may be able to hear a murmur in the large artery leading to the brain. Noninvasive tests have become available in recent years—that is, tests using ultrasound or other methods to determine the presence of a diseased or arteriosclerotic carotid, which could produce such attacks.

The cerebellum is located at the back of the brain and controls the body's equilibrium. If a *brain hemorrhage* is present in this area, the headache will be sudden and severe, located in the back of the head or neck. It is almost always accompanied by severe dizziness or vertigo, and the patient may not be able to stand up. Also, the headache may be accompanied by rigidity of the neck. This most often occurs in older people with no history of injury and usually precedes a coma. There is a flaccidity or lack of tone paralysis on the side of the body where the stroke has occurred. It is imperative to recognize cerebellar hemorrhage because neurosurgical procedures can prevent death.

A headache due to a ruptured or leaking *brain aneurysm* (a ballooned or weak blood vessel) is severe, often unbearable, and accompanied by neck stiffness. It usually occurs at the front of the head and usually affects younger individuals, although it can occur at any age. There is bleeding into the spinal fluid, and therefore the affected person will have a marked rigidity of the neck or meningitis-like symptoms. The headache is intensified by movement. It starts suddenly and may become catastrophic within minutes as the patient loses consciousness, has an epileptic seizure, or dies. The patient may be brought into the emergency room in an unconscious state with neck rigidity. It was once thought that one-sided headache was due to an aneurysm, but this is not true. There is no association between headaches and aneurysms or blood vessel malformation. Sometimes the bleeding is minor and the doctor can do necessary blood vessel visualization to find the aneurysm and then correct it surgically. Since blood in the spinal fluid is an important diagnostic clue, this is one of the few instances when spinal puncture is indicated for a headache patient.

Usually the headache of *meningitis or encephalitis*, which is an infection of the spinal fluid in the coverings of the brain, is insidious in onset over several hours or days. The headache is bilateral over both sides of the head and extends down the neck and becomes worse with head movement. Neck stiffness and rigidity gradually develop. In any child who has fever associated with headache, meningitis or encephalitis should be suspected, unless the child has a definite history of migraine. As the infection increases, the pressure within the head will also increase and the headache becomes diffuse, often beginning in the back of the head and radiating to the front.

In order for *hypertension* to cause headache symptoms, a person generally must have severe and disabling high blood pressure. The headache is usually dull, with a pounding component. Stooping or bending over will tend to increase the pain. The blood pressure must be over 200 mm Hg systolic and 120 mm Hg diastolic to cause these symptoms. A tumor of the adrenal gland (pheochromocytoma) is rare, although it can mimic migraine and give episodic elevations of blood pressure. People who get headaches due to excessive hypertension should be managed with antihypertensive drugs.

Normal pressure hydrocephalis is a condition that usually affects older people. Dementia or senility accompany the headache. A CAT scan reveals atrophy of the brain and increased size of the cavities or ventricles which contain the spinal fluid. A spinal tap will usually reveal no increase in pressure. A shunt which relieves the spinal fluid pressure can help many of these patients.

Temporal arteritis is life-threatening because it can lead to blindness. It is usually a one-sided, intense, deep, aching, persistent, throbbing or burning type of headache. The pain is worse when the patient is lying flat in bed. Chewing usually increases the intensity, and it is also made worse by stooping. Most often the patients are over age 60. It is important to recognize that the arteries may be distended and the region where the superficial artery reaches the scalp may be reddened. There will also be increased sensation in the scalp. Loss of vision may accompany the headache. Early diagnosis is essential to avoid blindness. Temporal arteritis can be readily treated by the administration of steroids.

We have already discussed cluster headaches. It must be emphasized, however, that cluster headaches can be so severe and disabling that the patient becomes suicidal because of the attacks. This is the reason that it is imperative for a cluster headache patient to seek and receive immediate treatment.

Although life-threatening headaches are rare, anyone with a headache problem, especially one of recent onset, should be aware of organic causes which need urgent treatment. The headache sufferer should be aware of the following six danger signals:

1. A headache that fails to readily form an innocuous pattern. That is, a headache that interferes with a person's life and prevents him from normal activities.

2. A headache that starts late in life or in early childhood. A thorough investigation is imperative in order to rule out any organic causes.

3. A headache with a recent onset. That is, a headache that occurs for the first time in a person who does not present a long history of headaches. Again, a thorough general examination is indicated.

4. Any neurological symptoms such as temporary

loss of or change in vision, motor function, or sensation. Further investigation is required.

5. A headache that does not follow a normal pattern. This deserves special testing.

6. Any abnormal physical signs, such as stiff neck or fever accompanying the headache, or an excessive intake of pain-relieving drugs. This warrants further investigation.

12

WHAT SHOULD YOU DO ABOUT YOUR HEADACHE?

Analgesics

Analgesics can be used effectively to treat the occasional headache. There are various combinations and types of analgesics. They can be found in a simple form, such as aspirin or acetaminophen, or combined with caffeine, antihistamines, decongestants, stomach buffers, or narcotics. Analgesics raise the pain threshold, thereby reducing the sensation of pain that is felt. Aspirin and acetaminophen are the most commonly used pain relievers.

Plain aspirin is the least expensive, most effective non-prescription analgesic. It can reduce fevers and inflammation as well as raise the pain threshold. Aspirin is acetylsalicylic acid and, because it is acidic, cannot be tolerated by some people. It may be combined with buffers that minimize the effect of the acid. Taking aspirin with liquids may also minimize the effects of the acid on the stomach lining. It should not, however, be taken by people with stomach disorders such as ulcers or gastric bleeding. Aspirin should also be avoided by people taking anticoagulants or diabetic medications. Aspirin must be carefully used for occasional head pain and never for recurrent pain. Large doses can cause various side effects, including stomach distress, giddiness, and ringing in the ears.

Acetaminophen, like aspirin, will lower a fever as well as raise the pain threshold. It does not, however, have anti-inflammatory capabilities. Acetaminophen (Tylenol, Datril) is not an acid; thus, it does not cause stomach damage. However, excessive use can lead to liver damage.

Combination drugs may also be useful. Caffeine is often combined with analgesics, with Anacin being one such preparation. Excedrin contains aspirin, acetaminophen, caffeine, and salicylamide, another pain reliever, which is thought to be less effective. Aspirin, caffeine, and phenacetin, another less effective analgesic, are combined in APC and ASA compound. Caffeine may help constrict the blood vessels and help the analgesic to be absorbed, as well as act as a stimulant. Other combination analgesics such as Bufferin, Cope, and Vanquish include buffers like aluminum hydroxide, magnesium hydroxide, sodium bicarbonate, and magnesium carbonate. Antihistamines may be found in some analgesics as they can add anti-inflammatory properties to the analgesic and help with sleeping as well. Excedrin P.M. and Percogesic contain acetaminophen combined with antihistamines such as pyrilamine or phenyltoloxamine. Codeine or another narcotic combined with any of the simple analgesics may strengthen their effect on pain. The combination drugs are disproportionately more expensive than plain analgesics. Many contain ingredients that have been found to have little pain-relieving ability. Some combination medications are effective primarily because of the analgesics contained in them and not because of their added substances.

Analgesics will usually have little effect on chronic headache problems such as migraine or muscle contraction headaches. They should not be taken too frequently and certainly not every day. Generally two analgesic tablets taken in a four-hour period will provide the maximum relief that can be obtained from them. If more is needed to relieve the headache, then the analgesic is most likely not an effective treatment for that headache. A physician should be consulted at this point, as the headache problem will probably require more potent forms of therapy. A physician should also be consulted if the headache problem comes on suddenly in a normally headache-free person, if the headaches become frequent and severe and disrupt one's life, if the sufferer is a child, or if the headache follows an injury or blow to the head, or loss of consciousness. A headache associated with confusion, convulsions, fever, or pain in one of the organs such as the eye, ear, or jaw, also warrants medical consultation. Headache sufferers may want to contact the National Migraine Foundation,[1] which will provide information about headaches and supply a list of doctors who specialize in treating headache problems in different geographical areas.

Selection of a Physician or Clinic

Some headaches are best treated by the patient's general physician, while others are best handled by a headache specialist, neurologist, or psychiatrist. Again, the headache sufferer may wish to contact the National Migraine Foundation (see fn. 1). In any case, the physician should be sympathetic to the headache problem. In the past it was common for doctors to dismiss a headache problem as "being all in the sufferer's mind." Currently, however, many physicians have become interested in headache pain and finally believe that the pain is real and not imagined. Since they believe that the pain is real, they will search for its cause and cure rather than deny its existence. The modern family practitioner or internist may

---

[1] Questions on headache problems, headache clinics, and physician referrals should be addressed to the National Migraine Foundation, 5252 N. Western Avenue, Chicago, Illinois 60625.

be quite knowledgeable in treating headaches. The headache specialist, however, has seen a wide range of headache problems and his experience is primarily in this area. He usually sees the most difficult and perplexing headache disorders. He will stay with a headache problem, trying various therapies until it is brought under control—it can take months or years to find the appropriate therapy for an individual sufferer. Most important in solving any headache problem is a good rapport between patient and physician. Insight into the sufferer's personal life, both emotional and physical, is often helpful in bringing the headaches under control. The sufferer should also have confidence in his physician and the patience to work with the different medical combinations and treatments required.

Solving the Headache Problem

A complete, detailed headache history should be taken from each headache sufferer. It is often difficult to obtain an accurate history. Patients may find it helpful to make notes describing the headache's characteristics, symptoms, and pattern. These notes can help the physician to better understand the sufferer's particular disorder. The more information about the headache the sufferer is able to relate, the more likely a correct diagnosis will be made. Persistence in exploring the patient's past history is important in determining all of the factors implicated in his syndrome. Any detail may be relevant, and just allowing the patient to talk may lead to the discovery of some headache components or precipitating factors of which the patient was not aware. Thus, the patient must actively participate in his own treatment. Success in solving a headache problem depends to a large extent on the degree of cooperation between patient and physician. The headache sufferer should not try to treat his own headache.

As described in Chapter 4, the headache history first involves a precise description of the headache, including the onset or specific time of life when the headache began, the length of the problem, and the location, frequency, duration, and severity of the pain. The number of types of headache should be ascertained. It is also important to find out if there is any pattern to the headaches' occurrence, such as a specific time of day or a seasonal, menstrual, or obstetrical relationship. Aura or warning signs, associated symptoms, sleep habits, precipitating and aggravating factors, and emotional factors, such as the patient's relationship to his job, family, and friends, should be included in the headache history. Environmental stress and sexual habits may also be important. The history should contain a family medical history, the patient's own medical history (particularly relating to recent head injuries), and a surgical history. Any history of diseases of the eyes, ears, nose, throat, teeth, or neck and any allergies or sensitivities to drugs are important to note. One also wants to discover any previous testing that a patient has undergone. If the sufferer has recently completed a thorough checkup, it would not be beneficial to subject him to another battery of tests, and it may even be detrimental. Finally, the headache history should include any previous and current medications or other relief measures that the sufferer has tried and their degree of effectiveness.

A complete physical and neurological examination should follow the history. A general physical examination can reveal many illnesses that precipitate headaches. In addition, an examination of the patient's mental state, which involves the completion of various mental tasks, should be conducted. A careful examination of the head, the cervical spine, cerebellar functions, and reflexes should be performed. A motor function examination, testing strength and coordination, as well as a sensory function examination, testing one's reaction to various stimuli, should be included. The complete neurological examination should also involve a careful check of the cranial nerves which are responsible for sight, hearing, smell, taste, and face and jaw movements and sensations.

A headache disorder is rarely "cured." The goal is usually to reduce pain and bring the headaches under control. It may be a lengthy process, as the physician first tries to reduce the pain and then attends to the root of the headache. Also, it is generally a good idea to persist with one physician even if the first form of treatment is not successful. He will then be able to proceed to the next sequential treatment, while, with a new physician, the sufferer would have to start all over again. Solving a headache problem may involve months of trying one therapy after another until the appropriate one is found. If a physician is unable to diagnose and treat a particular headache disorder, he may refer the sufferer to a headache specialist.

Solving the headache problem also involves a certain amount of "unlearning" of the pain response. Chronic headache sufferers tend to grow accustomed to a certain family response to their headache problem, and enjoy the added attention and sympathy. There are two sets of factors influencing chronic pain—organic factors and learned factors. The learned factors can lead to a pain habit, and the pain may continue after the organic cause has been eliminated. This is another aspect of the headache that must be considered. Family and friends should be advised not to reinforce this pain-related behavior. Well behavior should be reinforced by the physician and the sufferer's family and friends.

Necessary Tests

Since headache is a symptom of many organic diseases, some testing is generally warranted, particularly for patients being seen for the first time with a headache complaint. Many of the tests are conducted to rule out organic causes for the headaches. Only those tests essential for making a correct diagnosis should be performed. Most of the routine ones can be done in the physician's office. However, when the results indicate the need for further testing, hospitalization may be required. Many chronic headache sufferers go through extensive diagnostic testing, with some being tested to excess. If the patient has had a recent complete checkup, more testing is probably not necessary. Most records can be forwarded from one physician to another. Further testing may be detrimental, especially to the patient's attitude.

Routine blood tests and a urinalysis are generally done. A blood test checks for anemia or any infections that may be causing the headaches. The erythrocyte sedimentation rate is checked, to detect anemia or temporal arteritis. The blood pressure is checked, as an elevated blood pressure can increase the severity of the headaches. A urinalysis can detect kidney problems or diabetes, which can also worsen headaches.

There is no laboratory or x-ray test to diagnose the most common types of headache, that is, muscle contraction, migraine, and cluster headaches. When the symptoms are typical of one of these types or when the physical examination is negative, there is probably no need for further investigation. Many doctors will confirm their diagnosis by following the patient over a number of months or years and observing his response to treatment. Many physicians, even with all the criteria satisfied, will perform investigations solely to reassure the patient that there is no ominous cause for the headache.

If available, contrast-enhanced computerized axial tomography is the single most reliable way to identify an intracranial lesion. A CAT scan will identify most baseline lesions such as brain tumors, subdural hematomas, and abscesses. It will also reveal hydrocephalis (increased pressure in the spinal fluid), as well as congestion of the brain. A CAT scan can detect arteriovenous malformations but is not very accurate in detecting aneurysms. However, this is not a major shortcoming because malformations and aneurysms seldom produce headaches unless they rupture. If bleeding occurs in the brain substance or cerebrospinal fluid, it is readily seen on the CAT scan. Scanning is basically a very safe investigation, although the intravenous contrast media may cause allergic reactions in some people.

Skull x-rays will show if there is increased intracranial pressure or pituitary disease. If there is a tumor, the x-rays may reveal a shift away from the midline. Increased markings may show evidence of arteriovenous malformations. However, in the majority of headache patients, skull x-rays are normal.

An electroencephalogram, or EEG, often reveals false negatives and false positives. The EEG tracing may not pick up tumors; it may be interpreted as normal when a lesion is present. If a clear-cut, one-sided abnormality is noted, the EEG findings should encourage the physician to undertake a more thorough investigation.

Isotope brain scanning is more reliable. It will detect most cerebral tumors larger than two centimeters in diameter. Smaller tumors are unlikely to cause headache unless they obstruct the cerebrospinal fluid system. This is not a very accurate method for detecting tumors in the back of the head. However, brain hemorrhages due to trauma will be very evident. The frequent use of the brain scan has decreased since the advent of the CAT scan.

Few neurological tests are done with more enthusiasm and less indication than lumbar puncture. The only legitimate reason for doing a lumbar puncture on a patient with headaches is to confirm or refute a reasonable suspicion of hemorrhage or meningitis. The risk is great as it could cause the brain to herniate into the neck, resulting in sudden death in many patients.

Cerebral angiography is a method of observing the blood vessels while injecting the carotid artery. It carries about a 1% morbidity and tenth of 1% mortality risk. It is definitely indicated for subarachnoid hemorrhages in order to identify the underlying aneurysm or arteriovenous malformation. The CAT scan has more or less replaced angiography in investigating the possibility of tumors, subdural hematomas, and hydrocephalis. Angiography may be helpful in substantiating the suspicion of a transient ischemic attack from stroke or narrowing of the blood vessels leading to the brain. However, the use of Doppler studies and other noninvasive techniques is preferred to angiography for this purpose.

Pneumoencephalography is a technique in which air is injected into the spinal column and the brain while it is visualized with x-rays. Lumbar puncture is part of the procedure. There is some danger from this test, and it too has been replaced by the CAT scan.

Avoiding the Drug Trap

Many people with chronic headache problems treat themselves for years by taking over-the-counter headache remedies. Recurrent headaches often lead to abuse of pain relievers and tranquilizers. People with severe, chronic headaches usually take more than the recommended dosage of analgesics; they tend to take more and more tablets in an attempt to find relief. This abuse rarely occurs with sufferers of organic pain-producing diseases, however. For some patients, analgesics act as mild stimulants, which can result in their abuse and habituation. Excessive use of analgesics may mask the headache symptom, thus making it difficult to diagnose the true problem.

Analgesics should not be taken on a continuous basis. If two tablets do not provide relief, taking two more will not increase the pain-relieving action. Two analgesic tablets will provide the maximum pain-relieving action for a three- to four-hour period. Generally, the more analgesics taken, the greater the pain when their effect wears off. A tolerance to the analgesic may occur and it may lose its pain-relieving ability. As plain aspirin rarely provides relief, the sufferer often relies on combination drugs that contain potentially harmful substances. When headaches become chronic, one should seek medical advice rather than prescribing more pills for oneself.

Excessive quantities of analgesics can be toxic. They can cause nausea, vomiting, giddiness, diarrhea, buzzing in the ears, or skin rashes. Habitual intake of analgesics over years can lead to permanent kidney damage. Patients who reach this point must stop taking analgesics completely. As many as 20% of patients who abuse analgesics exhibit gastrointestinal bleeding. Abuse may also be related to peptic ulcers or reduced red blood cell production, as in chronic anemia.

Antidepressants, tranquilizers, and various antimigraine medications can also cause problems if taken in excess. Even patients under a physician's care can be found taking excessive amounts of their prescription medications. Tranquilizer abuse can cause sedation or depression. Excessive use of migraine medications containing ergotamine tartrate may result in circulatory problems or changes in the heart rate or blood pressure. Ergotamine abuse is a particular danger with migraine sufferers using the drug every day. Many believe that their headaches will reoccur if they do not take their ergotamine tartrate. However, the reason that the headaches recur so often is the constant use of ergotamine. A vicious cycle results from ergot abuse. A short hospitalization may be necessary to interrupt the cycle and end the ergot dependency, as ergotamine tartrate can damage the blood vessels. Side effects from ordinary use include nausea, vomiting, diarrhea, excessive thirst, other gastrointestinal disturbances, and tingling or cramping of the extremities. With chronically excessive use, however, major circulatory changes can occur. The extremities may become cold, pale, numb, sweaty, and even gangrenous. Electrocardiogram changes may also be present. The excessive use of caffeine, a vasoconstrictor, may also lead to a rebound headache. Caffeine causes the blood vessels to constrict but as the effect wears off, they again dilate, causing a dull headache. This leads to the ingestion of more caffeine-containing substances, resulting in an abusive cycle.

If a headache sufferer consistently takes over 100 analgesic tablets in a month, more than 20 Darvon or codeine-containing tablets per week, more than 10 milligrams of ergotamine tartrate per week, or constantly uses habituating drugs such as sedatives or tranquilizers, he is absorbing an excessive amount of drugs. A patient may be habituated to his medication if he finds a need for the medication itself rather than its pain-relieving qualities. If a headache sufferer with a drug dependency consults a physician, the dependency itself must be treated before the headache problem can be attacked. Hospitalizing the patient, and thus putting him in a controlled environment, may be the best way to accomplish this end.

One way the physician can help the patient avoid drug dependency is by prescribing only small quantities of a medication. Many physicians dealing with pain will not prescribe addictive drugs unless it is absolutely necessary. Narcotics should not be prescribed for a person suffering from recurrent headaches. When the pain is chronic, not acute, the potential for drug abuse is quite strong. Drugs containing barbiturates are highly addictive. Another way to help prevent abuse or overuse of medication is to limit the number of refills of a prescription that a patient can obtain without seeing his physician. In this manner the physician can more closely monitor both the headache condition and the medication. No drug should be taken without close medical supervision. A medication may become unnecessary or the dosage may need to be changed, or a milder form of treatment may be all that is needed to control the headache problem. Thus, a continuing, close, and cooperative relationship is necessary between physician and patient.

13

QUESTIONABLE THERAPIES, OR HOW NOT TO TREAT YOUR HEADACHE PROBLEM

The headache sufferer often resorts to unconventional modes of therapy out of extreme pain and frustration. Some have traveled from physician to physician, trying one medication or treatment after another, unsuccessfully. They are exposed to hundreds of commercial advertisements for pain relievers or "miracle cures." Many turn to unscientific sources in an attempt to find some relief from their head pain.

Acupuncture

Acupuncture is an ancient Chinese art in which needles are inserted into various parts of the body to cure disease, especially diseases related to pain. The needles are inserted into the skin at specific sites and at varying depths and left in position for different lengths of time. Acupuncture is derived from the concept of differing forces in nature. When balance in the body is disturbed, disease is the result. Acupuncture is believed to restore the harmony in the body. Today it is a particularly popular but controversial type of therapy. Acupuncture may suppress the perception of pain, and it may help to relieve the pain of a specific headache. A number of acupuncture treatments may be necessary to obtain relief. It is not known how or why acupuncture is effective. The needles may interrupt the transmission of pain messages along the nerve pathways. Acupuncture does not affect the cause of chronic headaches, nor is it believed to prevent or "cure" a headache problem. Acupuncture must be used very selectively. Some patients are convinced that it is the only treatment for them. There may be a psychological component to acupuncture or "placebo effect," as the sufferer expects the technique to be effective. The overall effectiveness of acupuncture is yet to be assessed, as there have not been any well-controlled studies performed for evaluation.

Chiropractic Treatment

The scientific basis of chiropractic theory and treatment must be questioned. Many chiropractors are not trained to diagnose or treat medical disorders such as those associated with head pain. Since chiropractors believe that disease is the result of displaced vertebrae, consulting a chiropractor may delay the diagnosis of a serious medical problem. Manipulation itself may be dangerous in some instances. Some people claim to have gained some degree of pain relief after chiropractic treatment, particularly those patients whose headaches result from muscle contraction. However, most forms of treatment that relieve muscle spasms will help this type of headache problem. There are many claims that neck manipulation benefits headache patients, but it has not been shown to significantly reduce headaches.

Treatment for Hypoglycemia

Low blood sugar, although frequently blamed, is rarely the cause of a chronic headache problem.

Unnecessary Surgical Procedures

Throughout history migraine sufferers have been treated surgically. Very early in history trephining of the skull was used. In more recent years, the removal of teeth, tonsils, or even a gallbladder has been tried. Many women have undergone a hysterectomy in an attempt to relieve their headaches. At another extreme, surgical procedures have been carried out to cut the trigeminal nerve. Even surgery on the nerves of the temporal artery has been used to gain short-term relief, but it is of questionable value. Surgical intervention is of little or no benefit to the migraine sufferer. Blocking or sectioning nerves in the head and neck has also been tried unsuccessfully with cluster headaches. This may simply lead to the headache switching sides. A technique called cyrosurgery, where intense cold is applied to various arteries, has been used in the treatment of cluster headaches. It has helped some patients but is extremely controversial. Many headache sufferers have been advised that their headaches are caused by a deviated septum and that surgery is necessary. This is actually quite rare, and the headaches are generally not relieved by the surgery. Surgery is the most drastic form of headache treatment and probably the least successful. Surgical procedures should not be considered an appropriate form of treatment of chronic, recurrent headache problems unless there is a structural problem that is specifically causing the headaches.

Unnecessary Invasive Tests

A physician should order only those tests necessary for correctly diagnosing a headache problem. In most instances, it is possible to achieve this with totally safe procedures that are not invasive. Tests involving some risk should only be performed after other tests have proved them necessary for confirming or ruling out certain organic diseases. Unfortunately, some physicians use invasive testing indiscriminately.

It should be used only if a specific problem is suspected and less dangerous tests will not supply adequate information. For instance, a lumbar puncture is often done routinely, while it is extremely dangerous in the presence of a brain tumor. Thus, the physician must carefully consider each headache problem individually and order the appropriate tests for each particular circumstance.

Habituating Medication

It is extremely important for the physician not to habituate the headache sufferer to medication while trying to reduce the pain. He must watch closely for side effects, as well as signs of habituation to, the medications he prescribes, and he must be aware that all medications carry with them potential hazards. Many physicians who do not regularly deal with pain problems are not aware of the dangers of dependency on certain drugs used in the treatment of pain. Thus, the patient's need for medication must be carefully assessed and the risks versus the benefits weighed. Freedom from head pain that results in physical or psychological disability is not the goal of the physician or the patient.

14

HEADACHE TREATMENTS OF THE FUTURE

Polypeptides

Recent research has revealed that the brain produces chemical substances known as polypeptides. Two of these are described as enkephalins and endorphins, and react very similarly to morphine, one of the most important of the narcotic agents. Since migraine headaches cause such excruciating pain, it is not too surprising to discover that one of the major changes in the brain's chemistry occurs during this type of headache, and involves a decrease in the brain's own natural morphine-like substances, the enkephalins and endorphins.

Dr. Bruno Anselmi of Florence, Italy, and his colleagues examined cerebrospinal fluid samples from migraine sufferers who were experiencing a migraine attack, migraine sufferers who were not experiencing a migraine attack, and nonmigrainous subjects. The amount of enkephalin and endorphin chemicals, or pain-killing substances, in the spinal fluid was markedly lower in those experiencing the migraine attacks. In fact, the findings confirmed a decrease or even a complete

149

absence of morphine-like substances in the spinal fluid during migraine attacks.

Dr. Anselmi suggested that migraine may be due to a failure of the brain system that produces these polypeptides. His research team went one step further and took blood samples from migraine sufferers at the end of a migraine attack, from migraine sufferers not experiencing an attack, and from control subjects. The blood samples were examined to determine if the pain-relieving substances in the brain, the beta-endorphins, were present. It was found that the levels were significantly higher in the blood of the migraine sufferers at the end of the acute migraine attack. Dr. Anselmi and his group theorized that since the pituitary gland is known to release endorphins during stress, it is quite possible that a migraine stimulates the pituitary to release beta-endorphins. The production of synthetic beta-endorphins, and their administration to the patient at the onset of an acute attack, may be one of the therapies of the future for the migraineur.

Dr. Agu Pert, a researcher for the National Institute of Mental Health (NIMH), and his fellow scientists have reported evidence that acupuncture affects the production of these polypeptides or pain-killing chemicals in the brain. His results appear to demonstrate that acupuncture activates the endorphin and enkephalin systems. In a report to the British journal *Nature*, the authors describe the administration of electro-acupuncture to the ears of male rats. Following this procedure, examinations of the rats' brains revealed substantial depletion of endorphins in three brain regions and a concurrent increase in the endorphin level in the cerebrospinal fluid. Dr. Pert and his associates showed that during acupuncture, brain neurons release more endorphins, the natural painkiller. There are polypeptides, besides the endorphins or enkephalins, which have pain-relieving or opiate reactions, and these can also be released by acupuncture.

Newer Beta-Blockers

Propranolol (Inderal) was the first beta-blocker to be recognized by the Food and Drug Administration (FDA) for the purpose of prevention or prophylaxis of migraine. Its excellent action has been discussed earlier in this book. There are certain patients, such as those with asthma or those with diabetes mellitus, requiring treatment with insulin, for whom the use of this drug is contraindicated. For the diabetic patient, another drug has been approved by the FDA for the prevention of hypertension, but it has not yet been recognized for the prophylaxis of migraine. Metoprolol may offer relief to the migraine patient who is also receiving insulin therapy. This drug may also be used for the migraine patient who is asthmatic, where the use of propranolol is contraindicated. There will be an occasional patient who reacts to propranolol (Inderal) with vivid visual hallucinations or disturbing dreams. These patients may be tried on another beta-blocker, nadolol, which is now available in the U.S., for other types of treatment. However, except in these special instances, propranolol remains the drug of choice for the prevention of migraine.

Heparin and Anticoagulants

Dr. Ernst Thonnard of St. Elizabeth's Hospital in Washington, D.C., has completed some interesting research. His studies have revealed that a series of intravenous injections of heparin, a drug which decreases the clotting ability of the blood, may help decrease the number of acute attacks in patients with long histories of frequent headaches. Dr. Thonnard drew blood samples of migraine patients during acute attacks. The blood was drawn from either the earlobe or the temple on the side affected by the migraine. He studied the blood cells and their characteristics, specifically the basophilic leukocytes in these samples. Since these basophils are the blood cells that transport heparin, he associated a possible link to the migraine process.

Dr. Thonnard's studies revealed that an injection of serotonin into a migraine patient caused an increase in the circulating basophils, whereas in nonmigrainous patients there was a decrease. Also, an injection of norepinephrine, an adrenalin-like analogue, caused a significant increase. If he administered heparin a half-hour before the injection of serotonin or norepinephrine, however, the differences between the cell response of the migraine patient and the control subject disappeared. Dr. Thonnard further observed that the heparin interacted with some of the chemical compounds considered to be implicated in migraine and suggested that heparin may contribute to the spontaneous termination of migraine. These studies were based on data collected on 25 patients who received 2,500 to 5,000 units of heparin intravenously, on a weekly basis. The total number of injections ranged from three to 25, with an average of seven. Twenty patients showed substantial improvement. Dr. Thonnard has recently administered heparin by inhalation method and demonstrated similar results. The findings of these studies may be implemented clinically in the future. The consumption of Szechwan prepared foods, which contain an anticlotting substance and can cause hemorrhaging into the skin and other organs, may also decrease the number of migraine headaches in an affected person. This factor seems to confirm some of the findings of Dr. Thonnard.

Calcium Antagonists

In Europe, a group of drugs known as calcium antagonists has been used to treat patients with stroke and heart attacks. Their use in coronary artery disease and heart attacks is due to their preventing calcium, selectively, from causing the blood vessels of the brain and heart to constrict. Initially, in every migraine attack, whether it be classical or nonclassical, there is a constriction and then swelling of the blood vessels. The calcium antagonists have been used in Europe with some success in treating migraine attacks by preventing the initial vasoconstriction. They are now being tested selectively in the United States.

L-Tryptophan

A lack of a form of serotonin 5-hydroxytryptophan increases pain sensitivity; thus, a method of combating this condition would be to increase the concentration of this substance. However, it does not enter the brain when taken orally. Another amino acid, L-tryptophan, does enter the brain, where it develops into 5-hydroxytryptophan with the assistance of enzymes. Thus, a large amount of L-tryptophan will increase 5-HT levels. L-tryptophan has been tried in the treatment of migraine; however, the results in this country have been very disappointing. It has very few side effects, but it has not proved effective.

Clonidine

Drugs blocking the alpha effect of adrenalin-like analogues on the blood vessels would also be expected to help in the treatment of migraine, basically by slowing the initial vasoconstriction and thus preventing the attacks from developing. A drug used recently in Europe, Indoramine, has had some success in this regard. Also, clonidine (Catapres) has been somewhat effective. It is now being used in the therapy of certain drug addicts to help them overcome their addiction problem. Thus, it may be beneficial for the habituated migraine patient.

Pizotifen

Pizotifen (Sandomigran) is a powerful antiserotonin and antihistamine agent. According to some European researchers, after two weeks of taking the standard dose of three tablets per day, 80% of the patients note a decrease in the frequency and severity of their migraine headaches. This drug also has a potent antidepressant effect. However, this drug will probably not be approved in the U.S., as double-blind trials have not proved at all conclusive. Side effects include drowsiness and weight gain.

Platelet Antagonists

Investigators in Houston, Texas, have shown that there is a chronic clumping of blood cells in migraine patients which is unrelated to the type or the severity of the migraine attack. They have also reported an increased stickiness to the platelet during the acute headache phase of migraine. This is accompanied by an increase in the blood serotonin levels during the onset of the acute headache and subsequent decreases in the serotonin levels during the headache phase. This study suggests that some alteration in platelet clumping is responsible for the observed changes in the chemistry of human subjects. Therefore, it is believed that the use of drugs to prevent the platelets from aggregating or clumping may be of value in migraine, as it is also presumed to be helpful in strokes or certain heart conditions. The drugs described as platelet antagonists are commonly used: acetylsalicylic acid (aspirin), sulfinpyrazone (Anturane), fenoprofen (Nalfon), and dipyridamole (Persantine). These drugs act by lengthening the time that the platelets live, inhibiting their clumping to various substances, and preventing their breaking up. The therapeutic dose of aspirin is one tablet twice per day, sulfinpyrazone 200 mg two to four times per day, fenoprofen 300 mg three times per day, and dipyridamole 150–300 mg per day, in divided doses and taken with aspirin. There are many studies on the use of platelet antagonists. However, they have not been found to be clinically effective in the therapy of migraine patients.

HEADACHE GLOSSARY

Abdominal migraine: A type of migraine, in which the pain is over the upper part of the abdomen and lasts a few hours. It is most common in female children. Diagnosis is easily made because of the family history of migraine, the infrequency of the attacks, and the frequent simultaneous occurrence of headache. If it remains undiagnosed, however, the patient may be subjected to unnecessary surgery for abdominal complaints. (*See also* Migraine equivalent.)

Acoustic neurinoma: A nonmalignant, slow-growing tumor involving the eighth cranial nerve. Headache is a late symptom of this disorder. Other symptoms include dizziness, loss of balance, nausea, and ringing in the ears. Once the headache develops, it grows progressively worse. Diagnosis is very simply made by special x-rays of the internal auditory canal. Most cases can be adequately treated, with the tumor removed by microsurgery (surgery performed with the aid of an operating microscope).

Acupuncture: An ancient Chinese procedure which blocks pain by stimulating nerves. It is based on the theory that a counterirritant (puncturing) prevents the painful impulses from traveling up the spinal cord and thereby blocks them. However, its effectiveness has been seriously questioned.

Aging: With age, there is usually a decrease in the number of migraine attacks. Many migraineurs who have had classical migraine headaches will exhibit only the aura or warning as they grow older.

Alcohol headache: A headache brought on by consumption of alcohol, a vasodilator, which causes the blood vessels of the head to swell. Migraine or cluster headache patients often list alcohol as a precipitating factor. A hangover from alcohol, occurring six hours or later after a drinking bout, is probably not due to the immediate effect of drinking alcohol but to the breakdown products when alcohol is metabolized. Alcohol can also contain many impurities known as congeners, which can cause the "hangover headache."

Alice in Wonderland syndrome: A vision of distorted figures or shapes that occurs as part of the migraine attack in certain sufferers. Lewis Carroll got many of his ideas for his book on Alice from the aura he experienced with his migraines.

Allergies: Headache patients may note an increase in headaches during or following an allergic episode because of the acute swelling of the nasal lining and accompanying passages. However, studies have tended to disprove the many claims of a relationship between allergies and headache.

Altitude headache: A headache that develops with travel to a higher altitude. The headache is severe and often mimics migraine. Change in altitude may also increase the frequency of migraine and precipitate an attack. Recent work has shown acetazolamide (Diamox) to be effective in preventing altitude headache.

Amines: Biological substances that are normally present in the brain and body and affect blood level functions. Some are found in foods, while others are produced by the body itself. Amines are known to affect mood behavior and blood vessel constriction or swelling.

Amitriptyline: An antidepressant frequently used to treat muscle contraction headache as well as post-traumatic headache.

It has some sedative effect and is most often effective in chronic pain syndromes.

Amphetamines: A group of drugs having a stimulant action on the central nervous system. They were used at one time in combination with aspirin and other analgesics to treat migraine. Although this combination is sometimes still used, most headache experts have not found it effective in the treatment of migraine.

Analgesics: Drugs that reduce the perception of pain by raising the patient's pain threshold. They are not cures for pain; they simply mask it. Analgesics range from plain aspirin or acetaminophen (Tylenol, Datril, etc.) to narcotics like morphine and Demerol.

Anaphylaxis: A severe allergic reaction in which the person goes into vascular collapse following the injection or ingestion of a substance to which he is sensitive. Symptoms include extreme irritability, shortness of breath, convulsions, loss of consciousness, and shock. Death may result. It is primarily caused by a contraction of the smooth muscle fibers. Rapid action by drugs such as adrenalin and steroids can prevent it. Severe allergic reactions like this rarely result from medicines used in treating migraine, but they may occur as a result of the dyes injected into the blood stream to visualize blood vessels in procedures such as arteriograms or computerized axial scans. A person with a previous history of allergies should be observed very carefully when using certain medications and during certain diagnostic procedures.

Aneurysm: A weakness in the blood vessel wall that balloons out and may rupture at some point. Aneurysms rarely cause symptoms before the rupture, unless they are large. They do not mimic the symptoms of migraine or cluster headache. It is vital to discover them before they rupture and have catastrophic consequences such as paralysis or death. (*See also* Cerebral aneurysm.)

Angioma (arteriovenous malformation): A hereditary type of blood vessel tumor consisting of interwining arteries and veins. The occurrence of the malformation does not appear to be more common in migraine sufferers than in the general population. There have, however, been reports of long-term remissions of migraine attacks in patients who have had large angiomas removed.

Antidepressants: Medications that raise the spirits of seriously depressed people. They focus on the emotion center of the brain and increase its use of certain chemicals present in the brain. Antidepressants elevate the level of the amines that are deficient in various mood and behavioral abnormalities. They may also have a beneficial anti-pain effect in certain headache problems even when depression is not present.

Anti-emetic: A drug used to prevent nausea and vomiting. It can be given orally, by injection, or rectally. Most of the drugs used as anti-emetics are phenothiazines.

Arteritis: A condition in which there is an inflammation of the blood vessels, often accompanied by vague muscle aches and pains. It occurs most often after age 55. If headaches occur in an older person for the first time, a condition such as arteritis must be considered. Early diagnosis is imperative since early treatment with steroids can prevent the secondary effect of the inflammation of the blood vessels—irreversible blindness. *(See also* Temporal arteritis.*)*

Arthritis: Arthritis of the neck area or cervical spine can be a cause of headache. An x-ray of the cervical spine will reveal some changes. If there is limited neck movement, plus articular crepitus (or grating of the neck), and pain in the neck and back of the head is present, arthritis should be suspected.

Asthma: Contrary to popular belief, there is no increase in the percentage of migraine headaches in asthmatic patients. However, if a patient has certain allergic reactions from desensitization or has side effects from some of the medications used in treating asthma, migraine-like symptoms can be exhibited by those with a predisposition toward migraine.

Atherosclerosis: A hardening of the arteries, in particular, a hardening of the arteries of the blood vessels supplying the brain. It can cause some symptoms of headache in the elderly.

Aura: *See* Warnings of migraine.

Barbiturates: A group of drugs that act as sedatives and are markedly habituating. Many popular headache medications contain a barbiturate. The primary objection to the use of these drugs is the possibility of addiction if the patient is taking these pain relievers on a daily basis. Intermittent use of these drugs is permissible.

Basilar artery migraine: A type of migraine that can occur in younger people, with the headache most often limited to the back of the head. The symptoms are caused by a diminished blood supply to the parts of the brain supplied by the basilar artery. Besides nausea, patients may have double-vision, unsteady gait, slurred speech and may seem confused. During the acute headache, many lose consciousness. Often these patients are mistakenly thought to be drunk or mentally ill. A previous history of migraine is helpful in making the diagnosis.

BC-105 (Pizotifen, Sandomigraine): A drug related to the tricyclic antidepressants. It is widely used outside the United States for the treatment of migraine. Careful testing in the United States has not revealed significant results.

Biofeedback: A method of treatment in which one is taught to control the body by feeding back the results of performance. With humans, the feedback is artificially mediated by man-made detection, amplification, and display instrumentation rather than being present as an inborn feedback loop within the biological system.

Biogenic amines: A group of substances that may control the brain's emotional status.

Blockers: Drugs that block the effects of adrenalin-related substances on the blood vessel walls and prevent the initial clamping down or vasoconstriction of the blood vessels, thus blocking migraine attacks. **Beta-blockers:** A group of drugs that block the action of adrenalin and its byproducts. Since adrenalin is produced by stress and affects the reactivity of the blood vessels, the use of these blocking drugs can be of some help in stress-related migraine. Propranolol (Inderal) is the beta-blocker most commonly used in the prevention of migraine.

Blood patch: A recent preventive measure, in which an injection of the patient's own blood into the site of a spinal puncture has proved successful in preventing post-spinal-puncture headache. After a spinal puncture, whether it is performed for diagnostic purposes or as a method of anesthesia, headache is a frequent complication, and has been a difficult condition to prevent and treat.

Brain abscess: Although rare, infection at any site in the body can be carried by the circulatory system to the brain and then develop in the brain or in the tissues surrounding the brain. When this occurs, it may remain dormant for many weeks or even years. Eventually, as the infection grows, the person will develop neurological symptoms. A brain abscess is often masked and may remain undiagnosed. It may result from infections of the sinuses and teeth, tubercular infections of the lungs, or minor skin infections. Differential diagnosis is made through the progression of symptoms, with headache and other neurological manifestations usually becoming progressively worse.

Butazolidin®: An antirheumatic substance which sometimes helps tension headaches. It must be used very cautiously because it can have an adverse effect on the blood cells. It has numerous other side effects.

Caffeine: A chemical substance naturally occurring in coffee, tea, and cola drinks. It is often combined with analgesics as well as ergotamine tartrate. Indeed, when combined with ergotamine, small amounts of caffeine are often helpful as a synergist in aborting migraine attacks. Excessive amounts of caffeine, however, can increase the number of headaches. Withdrawal from caffeine, as on weekends, can cause the "weekend headache."

Carotid angiogram: A procedure in which dye is injected into the carotid artery, a blood vessel located in the neck, in order to visualize the circulation in the head as well as in the brain itself. Angiograms were used frequently before the invention of the CAT scan. Carotid angiography is also helpful in determining a decrease in circulation to the brain due to hardening of the arteries.

Carotidynia: A migraine-like syndrome characterized by tenderness, swelling, and occasional pulsation of the carotid artery in the neck. This condition is frequently misdiagnosed. Its treatment is similar to that of migraine.

Catecholamines: Biologically active substances related to adrenalin that have a marked effect on the nervous and cardiovascular systems. The metabolism of these drugs may have some effect on migraine and has a definite effect on depressive headaches.

CAT scan: Computerized axial tomography produces thousands upon thousands of pictures. It utilizes x-rays which are combined by a computer into a single picture. This process enables the physician to make serial sections of the brain without invading the brain itself. It is used primarily to rule out organic disease as a cause of the headache problem. A CAT scan can be performed with or without dye. The dye may enhance the detection of a brain tumor or a blood clot.

Cerebral aneurysm: A condition caused by bleeding from a weakened or ballooned-out blood vessel. Most commonly it is hereditary. The headache resembles that associated with stroke and is of a very severe nature. Patients with an aneurysm require immediate treatment. If the blood vessel blow-out is not complete or of only a minimal degree, surgery can sometimes treat this type of hemorrhage successfully.

Cerebral atrophy: A condition in which the brain deteriorates. It is usually diagnosed by a CAT scan. The CAT scan will show marked enlargement of the brain ridges and the openings between them.

Cerebrospinal fluid: A clear, colorless liquid that cushions or protects the brain and spinal column. It increases or decreases in amount with the expansion or contraction of the brain. When the amount of spinal fluid is radically increased, it can cause headache. Usually, this increase is due to organic disease, but it can increase for no obvious reason.

Chinese restaurant syndrome: A condition named for the presence in Chinese foods of monosodium glutamate (MSG), which may produce a generalized instability of the blood vessels and thus cause headache, head sweating, or excessive abdominal cramps. Large amounts of monosodium glutamate should be avoided by patients who suffer frequent headaches. (*See also* MSG headache.)

Chronic paroxysmal hemicrania: A condition in which the patient gets multiple (15 to 20) headaches per day of short duration. It occurs primarily in women. These patients are responsive to therapy with an anti-inflammatory drug such as indomethacin.

Classical migraine: Differentiated from nonclassical or common migraine by the occurrence of a warning or aura prior to the acute attack. Many neurologists classify any migraine attack in which there are neurological manifestations as classical migraine. A migraine patient usually also has the following symptoms: nausea, or sick vomiting, a one-sided headache, a family history of headache, and a response to ergotamine tartrate (that is, ergotamine tartrate will abort the headache).

Cluster headache: A one-sided headache usually occurring in or around one eye and typically of short duration, usually lasting several minutes to several hours at the most. It is called cluster because it occurs in a group or series. The patient has tearing of the eye, nasal congestion, facial flushing, and constriction of the pupil on the side of the headache. The series may last several months, occurring more frequently in the fall and spring, and the headaches may disappear for several months or several years. Some forms of cluster headache, however, occur chronically.

Complicated migraine: A type of migraine headache associated with neurological manifestations. Although rare, permanent damage to the brain and the retina may be caused by migraine. Frequently, distortions of the visual field, paralysis, and anesthesia occur as residuals of these migraine attacks.

Confusional states with migraine: It is not uncommon in young migraine sufferers to find confusion and disorientation as a presenting sign of the migraine attack. Prolonged stupors or comatose states have been associated with migraine, lasting up to seven days.

Depression: This emotional state may be the cause of a daily, unrelenting headache which peaks in the morning and late afternoon. It is often accompanied by a sleep disturbance in the form of frequent and early waking. Migraine patients with frequent attacks often have depression as one of the complications of their migraines. Also, patients with chronic pain syndromes are often markedly depressed.

Dihydroergotamine: An injectable form of ergotamine tartrate which is very helpful to cluster or migraine patients and does not have as many side effects as oral forms of ergotamine tartrate.

Doppler Ophthalmic Test (DOT): A noninvasive test done with an instrument measuring blood flow to the superficial circulation of the eye. It determines if there is a decreased blood flow to the carotid arteries of the brain. This decrease may be significant since it may cause a small stroke and headache-like symptoms in older patients. Once identified, it can be readily treated.

Encephalitis: An inflammation of the brain itself, usually caused by a bacteria or virus, and a serious cause of headache. The bacteria type can be treated with antibiotics. The viral type may cause continual headache after the infection has subsided, as well as permanent neurological problems.

Endorphins and enkephalins: The most common bodily-produced polypeptides. Recently, it has been determined that the brain produces these morphine-like substances to counteract painful syndromes.

Epilepsy: Although an occasional epileptic patient will have a headache problem, there is no definite relationship between the two diseases. Often after an epileptic attack, however, a person will have a post-seizure headache. It is usually a generalized, moderate to intense, throbbing pain which is present for two to three hours after the seizure. Some scientists have reported that electroencephalographic changes are more common in migraine sufferers. However, the usual epileptic-type treatments are not of any help to these individuals, and most headache experts do not see epilepsy and migraine as related disorders.

Ergotamine: One of the drugs most frequently used to abort migraine. It is basically a vasoconstrictor, preventing the blood vessels from swelling. Since it does not decrease the cerebral blood pulse, it can be used for both classical and nonclassical migraine. The original drug comes from a mold that grows on rye, and the name is derived from the French word *ergot*. In the Middle Ages, eating bread made from moldy rye could be poisonous, causing gangrene of the hands and feet—a condition sometimes known as "St. Anthony's Fire." When the affected individuals went to St. Anthony's Shrine in Egypt, which was outside the infected area, they stopped eating the infected bread, and the malady was "miraculously" cured. Ergotamine has been discussed more extensively in Chapter 5 on Migraine Headaches.

Exertional headaches: With exercise, the muscles of the head, neck, and scalp require more blood and this causes a swelling or vasodilatation, which can cause head pain. Exertional headaches can, in some instances, be a sign of organic disease, and anyone that develops a severe headache following running, coughing, sneezing, bowel movement, or other exertions should certainly be checked to rule out any organic cause. The Diamond Headache Clinic has done extensive studies on both short and long-lasting exertional headaches. It has been found that those that are benign and not due to organic disease are responsive to therapy with the drug indomethacin (Indocin).

Extracranial: Referring to things outside the skull, scalp, and the muscles that cover the head.

Facial pain: Chronic facial pain can be very confusing both to the patient and physician. It is most difficult to treat and is frequently unresponsive to therapy. Patients with facial pain are easily habituated or addicted to analgesic medications. It may be caused by migraine-like syndromes, muscular syndromes such as TMJ, herpetic or rheumatic disease, or it may be purely psychogenic.

Glaucoma: A group of eye diseases characterized by increased pressure within the eye, which can cause headache. With a sudden and acute obstruction, the pain can be severe and terrifying. With a gradual increase of eye pressure, the pain may be more moderate in nature. Intraocular pressure should be measured in headache patients. This procedure can be performed in any physician's office. Drugs used to treat depressive headaches may, in rare cases of glaucoma, cause an increase in intraocular pressure if the canal in which the eye fluids drain is inadequate.

Glossopharyngeal neuralgia: A rare inflammation of the ninth cranial nerve (the glossopharyngeal nerve). The pain is intermittent and severe, and is usually described as being around one side of the tonsillar area, the outer ear, the back of the tongue, or the angle of the jaw. The attacks can be induced by coughing, talking, or swallowing. Treatment is similar to that for trigeminal neuralgia or tic douloureux and is usually effective.

Greater occipital nerve: The nerve that supplies the scalp and the back of the head. Because of its tortuous course between bone and muscle substance, it is particularly vulnerable to trauma and pressure. Since this nerve supplies sensation to the major portion of the skull, pressure on it can cause a headache-like syndrome, sometimes called suboccipital neuritis.

Head jolts: Certain headaches are particularly sensitive to head jolts because of swelling of the pain-sensitive blood vessels covering the brain. In this group are hangover headache, post-spinal-puncture headache, post-concussion headache, or headache associated with meningitis or inflammation of the brain. A headache due to a brain tumor can also be sensitive to head jolts. Migraine or muscle contraction headaches are usually not sensitive to jolting or position changes of the head.

Hemicranial: Refers to anything inside the covering of the brain or the skull.

Hemiplegic migraine: A very rare form of migraine in which there is paralysis of the arm or leg on one side of the body. The paralysis can occur before, during, or after the onset of a headache. There is frequently a family history of headaches with similar types of attacks. The attacks are usually temporary, but they may be prolonged and can cause some permanent paralysis.

Histamine: A normal substance present in the body, which is released if tissues are injured. Histamine has been implicated as one of the substances in the blood considered to be a causative factor in cluster headache, and it has also been considered a provocative factor in migraine headaches. If histamine is given to a migraine patient, it can provoke a migraine-like headache.

Horner's syndrome: Symptoms include drooping of the eyelids and constriction of the pupil with an injection to the white part of the eye, along with nasal congestion or drip. Some of these symptoms are also seen in cluster headache, or they can be a sign of severe neurological disease.

Hostility: Although not a primary cause, suppressed anger or repressed hostility can be a precipitant of migraine headaches. It is often but not always present in migraine-prone individuals.

Hot dog headache: A severe headache that usually starts within three-quarters of an hour after eating foods with sodium nitrite (used as a preservative in many meats, such as hot dogs, bacon, ham, and salami). It is added to prevent the bacteria of botulism and also to give a uniform red color to the meat. Migraine sufferers are more prone to this type of headache.

Hypertension or high blood pressure: Hypertension is not a common cause of headache unless it is a malignant type, with a systolic pressure of over 200 Hg and a diastolic pressure of over 110 Hg. Most of the headache complaints of patients with milder hypertension are probably related to severe anxiety over their illness or other external factors. If the headache is due to severe hypertension, it is usually worse in the morning and decreases in intensity as the day continues. **Benign intracranial hypertension:** A condition of increased intracranial pressure for which no specific cause is known. Usually, despite extensive laboratory testing, one cannot determine an obvious cause such as brain tumor, high blood pressure, etc. It may be due to menstrual dysfunction, hormone deficiency, hypothyroidism, or excessive intake of antibiotics or vitamin A. A prominent sign of this condition is marked congestion and distortion of the optic nerve as it enters the retina. The term "papilledema" is used to describe this state.

Hypnosis: A type of treatment in which the therapist puts the patient in a subconscious state. The objective manifestations of the mind become inactive, enabling the patient to relax and forget his head pain. Hypnosis has not been found to be an effective method of therapy for patients with cluster headache problems.

Hypoxia: A lack of oxygen which, coupled with an increase of carbon dioxide in the blood, has been observed to cause a swelling of the blood vessels of the brain. It is for this reason that some people get a headache at high altitudes. The headache often appears hours after exposure to low oxygen tension and is not relieved by the administration of oxygen. This factor has particular clinical significance because it has been theorized that low oxygen tension and hypoxia may be the initiating factor in all migraine attacks. A group of drugs, known as calcium antagonists, which will soon be available in the United States, act to prevent cerebral anoxia. These drugs may be effective in the prevention of migraine.

Ice cream headache: Ice cream lovers can experience intense, brief pain in the throat, head, or face after biting into ice cream or placing a spoonful against the back part of the roof of the mouth. The headache can occur when any cold substance is similarly positioned. The pain can be excruciating but disappears within a few minutes. Some investigators have reported that this type of headache occurs more frequently in persons who are prone to migraine.

Inflammation: A response of the body to irritation or injury. For example, in a migraine attack, accompanying the swelling there is a rush of various blood cells into the affected areas, producing redness, swelling, and warmth.

Lower half migraine: A type of migraine in which the pain is felt in the face or around the ear or even as low as the cheeks or jaw; or it may have a distribution similar to that found in cluster headache. The pain is often less severe, less sharp, and may last longer than regular migraine attacks. It is difficult to treat.

Meningitis: An inflammation of the brain coverings that is almost always associated with headache. The inflammation causes a stiff neck, which is typical of meningitis, and a high temperature. Immediate care is necessary. A spinal tap will usually confirm the diagnosis of meningitis and with modern antibiotics, about 99% of the cases can be cured. The headache is not chronic, but acute.

Menstruation: It is very common for a woman to get migraine headaches exclusively with her periods or at ovulation. A drop in estrogen levels during these times may be a precipitating cause. Menstrual migraine can be adequately treated with small doses of ergotamine or anti-inflammatory drugs prior to and during the woman's period.

Migraine equivalents: A term for migraine that exhibits itself in forms other than head pain. A diagnosis of migraine equivalent is determined by a previous history of typical migraine attacks, no evidence of organic lesions, and the replacement of normal headaches by an equivalent group of symptoms. It is important in these cases to determine the presence of a family history of migraine. Also, it is characteristic that drugs used to treat migraine will help the equivalent symptom. The most frequent migraine equivalent is "abdominal migraine," which is characterized by recurrent episodes of vomiting and abdominal pain without the symptom of headache. The bouts of pain can last anywhere from one to seven hours. Abdominal migraine occurs more frequently in female children. Patients characteristically show yawning, listlessness, and drowsiness during their attacks. Many persons with abdominal migraine have undergone unnecessary abdominal surgery. A migraine equivalent may also be characterized by visual symptoms such as blind spots, seeing half the field of vision, or loss of vision without the migraine headache. Another type of equivalent is psychic migraine, in which the patient exhibits transient mood disorders or erratic behavior as part of or in place of the headache syndrome.

MSG (monosodium glutamate) headache: It has been found that monosodium glutamate can cause headaches or other symptoms in susceptible people. It is often added to Chinese foods, with wonton soup a frequent offender. However, it is also found in many processed meats and tenderizers. Symptoms occur within 30 minutes of ingesting MSG, as it is rapidly absorbed by the stomach. Although the headache chiefly affects the temples, there may also be perspiration, tightness, and pressure over the face and chest. (*See also* Chinese restaurant syndrome.)

Muscle contraction headache (tension headache): A nonspecific headache, which is not vascular or migrainous, and is not related to organic disease. It is caused by a tightening of the muscles at the back of the neck and of the face and scalp. Muscle contraction headache is a steady, mild headache, and is sometimes described as having a bandlike or hat-band distribution around the head. It can occur episodically, that is, occasionally, or once or twice a month, and is usually best treated with simple aspirin or acetaminophen (Tylenol) compounds. The simple, episodic tension headache is often associated with fatigue and the stresses of life. These people rarely consult a physician for their headaches. Those who do seek the help of the physician have a chronic type of muscle contraction headache, which may be due to a psychological problem or to a masked or hidden depression.

Nicotine: The nicotine found in cigarettes and other smoking materials can increase the frequency and duration of migraine attacks. Excessive smoking can also be a factor in cluster headache attacks.

Nitrates and nitrites: Nitrates are used to treat coronary heart disease and nitrites are used as food additives to prevent botulism in meats. Both of these substances can increase vasodilation and thus increase the tendency toward migraine attacks.

Nonclassical migraine: A condition with the same symptoms as classical migraine, except the warning, or aura, is missing.

Ophthalmoplegic migraine: A rare type of headache that occurs in children or young adults. Associated with the headache, there is paralysis of the third nerve and there may be drooping of the eyelid, dilation of the pupils, and paralysis of the eye muscles. This is a temporary type of migraine, and patients usually have a family history of similar attacks.

Oral contraceptives: The estrogens in oral contraceptives and in post-menopausal hormones can increase the frequency, duration, severity, and complications of migraine. Any type of estrogen is contraindicated in most migraine patients.

Papilledema: A condition that occurs following an inflammation of the optic nerve at the point of entrance into the eyeball. On examination, inflammation or swelling of the optic nerve can be observed. It is usually caused by increased intracranial pressure but can be caused by a brain tumor pressing on the optic nerve. It is an excellent indicator for the physician seeking to determine an organic cause of headache.

Pheochromocytoma: A tumor of the adrenal gland which causes marked transient elevations of blood pressure and may provoke symptoms that mimic migraine disease. A simple blood or urine test can differentiate migraine from this disorder.

Placebo: A drug or treatment that has no medical benefit but whose success is related to the suggestion that it will work. Thus, placebo response refers to the beneficial effect that a placebo medication will have when given to certain individuals. It is estimated that about 25% to 30% of individuals will have a placebo response to drugs.

Platelet antagonists: A group of drugs containing a substance that prevents the platelets from disintegrating or clumping together. These drugs may have significance in the treatment of migraine since the platelets contain the chemical serotonin, implicated as one of the causes of migraine.

Polymyalgia rheumatica: A medical condition which usually occurs after age 55 in which there are marked muscular and rheumatic pains. Temporal arteritis, which can cause a severe form of headache as well as blindness, is one manifestation of polymyalgia rheumatica. It is essential to identify this condition for proper treatment.

Polypeptides: Amino acids which may have some pain and headache prevention qualities, but may also cause headaches. They are normally present in the brain. The ones being investigated currently are the endorphins and enkephalins, which are morphine-like substances.

Pregnancy: Migraine will usually disappear by the second month of pregnancy, only to reappear after the delivery of the baby. Migraine rarely occurs from the second month of pregnancy to birth because of hormonal changes.

Prolactin: A hormone released by the pituitary gland. There has been an increase in the number of cases of benign tumors of the pituitary gland with headache as one of the symptoms. It most often occurs in young adults. This hormone can be easily measured in the blood and, if markedly elevated, more sophisticated pituitary tests can be performed. An increase in prolactin is usually accompanied by an increase in breast size, discharge from the breasts, or irregular periods.

Prostacyclin: A substance similar to prostaglandin which is released by the wall of a blood vessel and has the opposite effect of prostaglandin. It prevents the platelets from aggregating or clumping together and may cause the blood vessels to dilate; therefore having a prophylactic effect on migraine headaches.

Prostaglandins: A group of approximately 14 chemical substances released by various organs. The first one identified was released by the prostate, thereby earning the name "prostaglandins." One prostaglandin in particular may provoke migraine by causing the platelets to aggregate or clump together, thereby causing a release of serotonin. These substances also have a marked effect on the blood vessels and smooth muscles and are part of an inflammatory reaction. Thus, prostaglandin release can be a causative factor in headache, and substances that negate the action of prostaglandins can help decrease the frequency, severity, and duration of headache.

Ptosis: Drooping of the eyelid, usually on one side of the head. It can be a sign of organic disease but most commonly is a symptom of cluster headache.

Raeder's syndrome: A syndrome similar to cluster headache and usually treated in the same way. Some practitioners would like to consider it a separate condition.

St. Anthony's Fire: A syndrome from the Middle Ages in which fever, redness, gangrene, and other symptoms appeared after the eating of moldy bread on which ergotamine had formed.

Scotoma: A blind spot of varying size which may occur within the field of vision. Scotomas are sometimes present with the onset of migraine headaches as part of the aura.

Sella: The cavity in the brain that encases the pituitary gland. When the cavity is enlarged or somewhat distorted, it can signify the presence of a brain tumor.

Serotonin: A chemical substance primarily present in the platelets. It is a potent constrictor of the blood vessels and is thought to be involved in the mechanism of migraine.

Sinusitis: The area affected by sinus headache is usually above the eyes (frontal sinus) or below the eyes (maxillary sinus). Headache very often follows an upper respiratory infection which blocks the sinuses. The pain is caused by a stretching of the lining of these open cavities and the formation of pus within the sinuses, which will not drain. Often the areas above or below the eyes, where the sinuses are located, are very tender. Chronic sinus disease rarely causes head pain. Acute sinusitis, associated with a fever and a blocked sinus, can cause acute head pain.

Skin or allergy testing: Not relevant in migraine diagnosis or therapy. Allergy desensitization is not helpful in migraine treatment.

Strokes: It is not true that migraine patients are more prone to strokes, even though certain strokes can produce headache as an initial symptom. Patients with a cerebral hemorrhage almost always have a headache, particularly as the blood enters the spinal fluid. However, this is only a transient type of headache and the stroke symptoms, such as paralysis, are the ones that predominate.

Temporal arteritis: A vascular disease characterized by inflammation of blood vessels, which produces a very severe headache and usually strikes people over age 55. The arteries in the temple are thicker and more tortuous than normal vessels. In some cases, patients may have other bodily symptoms such as loss of appetite, or joint and muscle pain. A simple sedimentation rate (blood test) will suggest this diagnosis because it is often quite elevated. A biopsy of the temporal artery, which lies just below the skin, confirms the diagnosis. It is important that the patient receive immediate treatment because the condition can lead to blindness.

Temporomandibular joint dysfunction (TMJ): This diagnosis is probably one of the most overused terms relating to head pain. Symptoms include localized facial pain, limited jaw movements, muscle tenderness, and sensations when moving the jaw up and down. Usually, x-rays of this joint are normal. The pain is most often described as being located in front, behind the ear on the affected side, and may radiate over the cheeks and face. Some people will complain of a sensation of blockage in the ear. Thousands of dollars have been spent on unnecessary procedures. The treatment is focused on relief of the muscle spasms by using simple tranquilizers or muscle relaxants. Moist heat massage is also helpful. However, dental splints are rarely helpful. Patients must be cautioned against extensive reconstructions of the mouth, since they are usually not indicated or helpful.

Tension headache: *See* Muscle contraction headache.

Third ventricle cyst: A rare, nonmalignant type of growth that blocks the spinal fluid from flowing on its normal route from the ventricles into the spinal cord. There is a narrow passage in the middle of the brain, where a cyst may prevent the normal flow of the fluid. The typical headache characteristic of this condition will occur during changes of position. Surgery is usually required.

Tic douloureux (trigeminal neuralgia): Episodes of severe shooting or stabbing pain on one side of the face which are generated by eating, talking, shaving, or cold drafts. The painful spasms last a few seconds and are severe and intolerable. Tic douloureux most commonly occurs after the age of 50 and is more frequent in women. It can be treated medically or surgically.

Tranquilizers: Medications that lessen anxiety, emotions, and tension. Many are habituating and, if used in elderly people, can cause some serious side effects.

Transcutaneous electrical neurostimulation: The use of electrical currents to alleviate headache pain. It has been used extensively in treating cluster and migraine headaches but has not proved to be an effective form of therapy.

Trigeminal neuralgia: *See* Tic douloureux.

Tumor: The greatest fear of all headache patients is that their headache is caused by a brain tumor. However, this is uncommon; only one-tenth of 1% of all headache patients suffer from a brain tumor. Their history consists of a recent onset of headache with increasing severity. The headache is made worse by exertion such as coughing, sneezing, or running, and the patient may exhibit some other neurological symptoms such as changes in handwriting, personality, and thought. Upon examination by a physician, there may be some defect in either motor, sensory, or brain reflex activity.

Tyramine: A naturally occurring substance in the protein of the body which is also found in certain foods and beverages. Ingestion of these foods can cause more frequent migraine attacks.

Vasoconstriction: A narrowing or a clamping down of the blood vessel.

Vasodilatation: A swelling or distention of a blood vessel.

Vasomotor rhinitis: A congestion of the nose which can be triggered by a variety of stimuli such as temperature change, exercise, change of position, humidity, and odors. It is rarely an allergic reaction. A patient may exhibit a mild headache with vasomotor-rhinitis-like symptoms.

Warnings of migraine: The warnings usually occur just a few minutes before the initial migraine attack. They may take the form of a feeling of elation, a clearer awareness of color, variations in mood, an increase in energy, or a feeling of hunger or thirst. Conversely, some patients may get a feeling of depression. Classical auras can be positive, as in visions of bright lights or stars, or lines resembling forts (known as fortification spectra), or they can be negative, as in seeing blind spots or only part of the visual field. The warnings may also distort figures or shapes (*see* Alice in Wonderland syndrome). Some people get tingling, pins-and-needles sensations in one arm or leg (paresthesias). Some describe a strange odor. All of these are the warnings, or aura, of migraine.

Weather-related headache: Studies conducted by a Swedish research group have recorded headache attacks in relation to climatic factors such as atmospheric pressure, outdoor temperature, wind velocity, cloudiness, relative humidity, and precipitation. An increased headache frequency was associated with high temperature, low pressure, and high wind velocity. It was concluded that climatic factors influence headache frequency.

APPENDIX: TYRAMINE-RESTRICTED DIET FOR HEADACHE SUFFERERS

Tyramine is formed by the chemical decomposition of tyrosine. Disorders of tyrosine metabolism may occur in patients taking certain monoamine oxidase (MAO) inhibitors (a type of antidepressant medication). These deactivate enzymes needed to metabolize tyramine. A tyramine-restricted diet helps prevent symptoms of severe high blood pressure, headaches, and nausea.

Tyramine content may vary among brand names available in the market because of preparation, processing, or storage. It is best to eat only freshly prepared foods and to avoid eating foods that may have been aged, fermented, pickled, or marinated. Tenderizers, monosodium glutamate, and nitrate or nitrite compounds are likely to be provoking agents. It is important to read labels carefully when shopping and to ask questions when eating away from home.

Sample Menu

This sample menu is intended to present a practical approach to limiting foods high in tyramine and to be helpful to

178

those primarily preparing food at home. Remember: (1) Ty-ramine content of foods may vary among brand names available because of preparation, processing or storage. (2) Limit banana and citrus fruit to ½-cup serving daily. (3) Decaffeinated coffee is not limited, but *do* limit regular coffee, tea, cola, or chocolate to 2 cups daily. (4) Do *not* use commercial canned soups. (5) Milk can be used as desired.

Breakfast	*Lunch*	*Dinner*
½ Grapefruit	Cranberry Cocktail	Fruit Punch
Choice of Cereal	Roast Turkey	Grilled Hamburger/Bun
Egg	Mashed Potatoes/Gravy	Catsup/Mustard (no
Bran Muffin	Broccoli	pickle or onion)
Jelly	Celery, Carrot Sticks	Corn on Cob
Butter or Margarine	Custard Pie	Sliced Tomato & Cu-
Milk		cumber
		Fresh Fruit in Season
Tomato Juice	Cottage Cheese Fruit	Beef Pot Roast
Choice of Egg	Plate	Browned Potato
Cereal	Rye Krisp or Muffin	Carrots
Milk	Butter or Margarine	Celery
White Toast	Sherbet	Gravy
Jelly		Lettuce Wedge/French
Butter or Margarine		Dressing
Milk		Fruit Crisp
Orange Juice	Home-Cooked Soup	Chilled Grape Juice
Choice of Cereal	Sliced Turkey Sand-	Broiled Lamb Chop
Egg	wich with 1 tsp.	Baked Potato/Butter
Wheat Toast	Mayonnaise (if de-	Spinach Greens
Jelly	sired)	Molded Jello Salad
Butter or Margarine	Tomato & Lettuce	Pound Cake
Milk	Chilled Pears	
Stewed Prunes	Baked Chicken	Home-Cooked Vege-
Choice of Cereal	Shoestring Potatoes	table Soup
Egg	Asparagus/Deviled Egg	Beef Ribs
Rye Toast	(½)	Oven-Browned Potato
Jelly	Citrus Fruit (½ cup)	Parsley Carrots
Butter or Margarine		Lettuce & Tomato Salad
Milk		Lemon Pudding

Breakfast	Lunch	Dinner
Grapefruit Sections	Spaghetti with Meat	Chilled Apple Juice
Choice of Cereal	Balls	Baked Pork Chop
Egg	Tossed Green Salad	Sweet Potato
English Muffin	with Dressing	Buttered Peas
Jelly	Fresh Fruit	Stuffed Prune with
Butter or Margarine		Cream Cheese Salad
Milk		Angel Food Cake
Orange Juice	Home-Cooked Soup	Chilled Tomato Juice
Choice of Cereal	Omelet/Mushrooms	Broiled Fish
Egg	Toast	Buttered Rice
White Toast	Potato Chips	Asparagus
Jelly	Sliced Cucumbers	Fruit Salad
Butter or Margarine	Canned Fruit	Ice Cream (no choco-
Milk		late)
Pineapple or Grapefruit	Chilled Salmon or Tuna	Sirloin Steak
Juice	on Lettuce/Cucumber	Baked Potato
Egg	Wheat Bread	Buttered Green Beans
Pancake/Syrup	Molded Jello Salad	Chef's Salad Bowl
Butter or Margarine	Rice Pudding	Fresh Strawberries or
Milk		Other Fruit in Sea-
		son

List of Permissible and Restricted Foods

Food Group	Foods Allowed	Foods to Avoid
Beverages	Decaffeinated coffee, colas containing no caffeine. Caffeine sources to be limited to 2 cups daily include coffee, tea, colas, and chocolate.	Alcoholic beverages, wines, ale, beer.
Milk	Homogenized, skim, 2%.	Chocolate, buttermilk.
Dairy Products	Cottage cheese, cream cheese, American cheese, Velveeta, or synthetic cheese. Yogurt in ½-cup portions or less.	Aged and processed cheese. Includes Cheddar, Swiss, Mozzarella, Parmesan, Romano, brick, Brie, Camembert,

Food Group	Foods Allowed	Foods to Avoid
		Gouda, Gruyere, Emmentaler, Stilton, Provolone, Roquefort, blue and cheese containing foods (pizza, macaroni and cheese). Yogurt and sour cream.
Meat and Meat Substitutes	Fresh prepared meats, eggs.	Aged, canned, cured, or processed meats, those containing nitrates or nitrites, commercial meat extracts, pickled or dried herring, chicken livers, sausage, salami, pepperoni, bologna, frankfurters, patés, peanuts and peanut butter, marinated meats. Any prepared with meat tenderizers, soy sauce, or yeast extracts.
Bread and Bread Substitutes	All except those on avoid list. Commercial bread.	Homemade yeast breads, fresh coffee cake, doughnuts, yeast, and yeast extracts. Sourdough breads. Breads and crackers containing cheese. Any containing chocolate or nuts.
Fruits	All except those on avoid list. Citrus fruits (oranges, grapefruits, pineapple, lemon, lime) are limited to ½-cup serving per day.	Canned figs, raisins, papaya, passion fruit, avocado, red plum, banana (½ allowed per day).
Vegetables	All except those on avoid list.	Italian broad beans, Fava beans, lima, navy and pea pods, sauerkraut, onions except for flavoring.

Food Group	Foods Allowed	Foods to Avoid
Desserts	All except fresh yeast-raised desserts or those containing chocolate.	Any with chocolate.
Miscellaneous	White vinegar. Commercial salad dressings in small amounts.	Brewer's yeast, chocolate, soy sauce, monosodium glutamate, meat tenderizers, papaya products. Accent, Lawry's, and other seasoned salts. Soup cubes, canned soups, frozen TV dinners. Some snack items and instant foods contain items to be avoided. Read all labels.

INDEX

Abdominal migraine, 60, 155, 169
Abscess, 3, 128
Acetaminophen (Tylenol, Datril), 85, 134-135
Acetazolamide (Diamox), 156
Acoustic neurinoma, 155
ACTH, 104
Acupuncture, 145-146, 150, 155
Adler, Charles, 116
Alcohol, 21, 30, 69, 71-73, 88, 99, 102, 114, 129, 156, 166
"Alice in Wonderland" syndrome, 58, 156
Allergy, 22, 52, 86, 99, 156, 157, 158-159, 174
Altitude headache, 156, 168
Amines, 69-71, 156, 159
  beta-phenylethylamine, 70
  see also Tyramine
Amitriptyline (Elavil), 89, 113, 120, 156-157
Amobarbital (Amytal), 115
Amphetamines, 34, 157
Amytal (see Amobarbital)
Anacin, 33, 135
Analgesic, 21, 31, 35, 85, 110-111, 115, 118-119, 120, 134-135, 142-143, 157
Anaphylaxis, 157
Anemia, 140, 143
Aneurysm, 27-28, 29, 51, 130, 157, 161-162

Angiography, 141-142
  carotid angiogram, 161
Angioma (arteriovenous malformation), 158
Anselmi, Bruno, 149
Antibiotics, 22
Anticoagulant medications, 129
Anticonvulsant drugs, 40, 60, 120, 123, 125
  carbamazepine, 123
  Dilantin, 120
Antidepressants, 34, 52, 86, 89, 113-114, 117, 154, 158
  amitriptyline (Elavil), 89, 113, 120, 156-157
  desipramine (Pertofrane), 113
  doxepin (Sinequan), 113
  imipramine (Tofranil), 113
  monoamine oxidase (MAO) inhibitor, 88, 113-114
  nortriptyline (Aventyl), 113
  protriptyline (Vivactil), 113
  side effects, 114, 143
  tricyclic, 113-114, 120, 123
Anti-emetic, 158
Antihistamine, 22, 24, 88, 135, 153
Anturane (see Sulfinpyrazone)
Anxiety, 30, 49, 109, 112
Anxiety headache (see Muscle contraction headache)
APC compound, 135
Aretaeus of Cappadocia, 10

183

propranolol, 86
Vasomotor rhinitis, 176
Vein, 29
Vertigo, 130
Vistaril (*see* Hydroxyzine)
Visual symptoms, 25, 58, 128, 132-133, 169-170
  see also Aura, Retinal migraine
Vivactil (*see* Protriptyline)
Vomiting, 19, 24, 57, 90, 119

anti-emetic, 158

Weekend headache, 31, 66, 73, 107, 161
  blood sugar level, 32, 33, 70
Whiplash, 124-125
Wigraine, 84
Wolpe, Joseph, 94-96, 116
Wolff, Harold G., 15-16, 125